PLAISIR D'AMOUR

"Pleasure Of Love"

By

POETRY PLANET

ISBN:
Hardbound-978-621-470-414-9
MOBI/KINDLE-978-621-470-415-6
Softbound/Paperback-978-621-470-416-3

Published by:
Poetry Planet Book Publishing House
Rosario, Pozorrubio, Pangasinan, Philippines
Contact Number: 09554960094
Email: maritesritumalta@gmail.com

CONTRIBUTING WRITERS

Afrose Saad
Akila Shariff
Alvin Agena Andino
Amb Maid Čorbić
Amiya Rout
Amrita Lahiri Bhattacharya
Amrita Mallik
Anjana Prasad
Anu Gupta
Asher Chipu
Asua Tyongi Gabriel
Azucena Libiran Gonzales
B.S.Saroja
Ben-hur Sistoso
Bernadette Lejarde
Besnik Lamaj
Boluwatife Alabi
Chandra Sekhar Batabyal
Chiedozie .I. Chinagorom
Churchil Ajunyia
Daniel Miltz
Davi Ramphal Rampersad
Deepa Vankudre
Deepti Shakya.
Deluke Muwanigwa
Dimithri Wijerathna
Dolo Rez
Dr.Sailabala Dash
Duška Kontić
Edmon Libres
Ency Bearis
Gatot malaisianto
Gina Gelua Maristela
Gloria A. Yu
Gloria Magallanes-Loeb
Gopal Sinha
Halima Khan
Halyna Bokoch
Harold Vite
Ivina Emmanuel Asoh
Izibetome Olisah Egbo
Jackson Agocha
Janet Rose Licudo
Jaya Karmalkar
Jem Maleon
Joscephine Gomez
Josh Hodgepodge
Jyotirmoy Ghosal
Kanduri Charan Rout
Karu Kala-Mohan Jamda
Kenneth Munene
Kerchia Festus Terlumun
Kirti V
Kishor Kumar Mishra
Lekeaka McRawlings
Liege Lord Lanre
Loreta C Bande
Lubna Ahmed
Lucy A. mendiola
Lynn Valaquio Garcia
Madhuri Kulkarni
Mafizuddin Chowdhury
Manmohan Rajbanshi
Margaret Karim
Maria Editha Garma-Respicio
Maria Elvira Fernandes Correia
Marion Remnant Parish
Marissa P. Esmeralda
Marivic C. Miranda
Marvin Marcelino
Mayyu Hamim
Medy Villapando
Mir Samsul Haque
Mohammed Rashid Ali
Mohammed Toyob Khan
Mousumee Baruah
Nandita De
Nathaniel D. Cruz

Ning Gaspi Gaton
Nishat Jabeen
Nooriyah Karimi
Obingo Wesonga
Ogundijo Segun Daniel
Oiray J.Kings
OiRay Jay
Okoi Amadiowei Jacob
Ollga Farmacistja
Palash Baran Das
Pamela Tennant
Pragyan Parimita
Nanda
Prajaranjan Panda
Prashanta Kumar
Samanta
Priti Dhopte
Rajani Mula
Ramesh Chandra
Pradhani
Rana Zaman
Ratanang Seepapitso
Ratikanta Samal
Rena Zaman
Rhoda Rumbaua
Rhoda Tomelden
Rhodora Garcia-Medina
Ritu Kamra Kumar
Rodrigo M. Dantay ,Jr
Ronel David
Rose Huy Woolket.
Saroja Krishnamurthy
Seema Heela
Seema Sharma
Shamain Simeon
Sharmistha Das
sihem cherif
Silviya Veselinova
Snežana Šolkotović

Sudha Dixit
Sujata Dash
Suveera Bellary Kusnur
Swati Das
Taferi M. Simon
Teresita Barrera
Tha Ono
Tiare Nopera
Ulma Taboada
uzo Nwamara
Vasudha Pansare
Vee Barnes
Vicente A. Valdez.Jr
Vijaya Sarmah
Vinod Singh
Yanita Asikasari
Yassin Okinyi
Zenaida Laragan Taloza

FOREWORD

Writers describe love better because they are gifted with abilities. Poets are best known to be the most passionate Created being on earth. And when they were told to write about love, they pen like they live in a dream world, their poetries were beautifully expressed filled with passions and tender emotions.

PLAISIR D'AMOUR, "The Pleasure Of Love" is actually an inspiration from Jean-Pierre Claris de Florian's poem in *Celestine* and the original version of the musical classical song "PLAISIR D'AMOUR" that became the title of this book.

PLAISIR D'AMOUR is an expression of intense love by means of poetry... Metaphorically explained in whirlpool and Kaleidoscopic emotions... Written by more than 130 poets from different part of the globe, united in one goal...to enhance their writing by means of collaborating...

So open the book and be enchanted inside a world these poets created using their wide imaginations...

Marites Ritumalta
CEO/Publisher/Compiler

TABLE OF CONTENTS

PLEASURE OF LOVE

YOU LOVE ME IN YOUR OWN WAY

You love me in your own way,
Without a backup and conditioning,
Every moment you show me how much
I mean to you,
It is called love, a spectrum of colored feelings...

You love me differently,
Without egoism and vanity,
Our luck has no face, nor resemblance,
We love each other the same during the days of
distress.
You love me the way I am,
Without illusions or comparisons,
This is why our life is miraculous and simple.

Each and every touch is like a promise,
a trace of thrill...
You love me when I am about to get ill,
And when the unpleasantness is knocking on the door.

Our love is like a protest
There's no future without it...
You love me in your own way,
And the emotions are reciprocated.

Every gesture of yours says how much you value me,
Every wink is colored with lust and wish...
Your love makes me a happy woman...

Serbia

YOU WHO PASSED THEM

You who passed them
the boundaries of the dream,
you who have turned into focus,
you who have come back
in the evening breeze,
take and give messages,
still from the bottom of my soul.
We how have we lost
our ties,
not even at the worst,
I tell you.
We have loved it
Even to be silent,
yes we are thirsty again.
Now that the miseries have multiplied
and in the lane
the despair in between,
Us as always,
We going to break the rules,
and another communication,
do ti zeme bese.
Now for the night
I walk around alone.
The fourth time the dog
On the asphalt,
and their echoes,
And perceive spaces far away.
Flashes were me
I say two or three words.
I can't keep up with them
with me and start
I talk to them for a long time.

I tell her about her eye,
that we are sailing even now.
For the one who left me so far away,
Kuturu is walking alone.

Albania

AMBROSIA

What's is the divine drink,
We don't know,
Love at first sight we drink through beloved's eyes though.
Love is so thrilling, a unique feeling, inexperienced before,
I was lucky enough to meet my first love by the sea shore,
We both met for the first time in one serene morning,
Silence echoed silence,
Though our heart were pounding,
more louder than howling sea waves,
Kissing the shore.
Mouth zipped, Eyes spoke.
You broke the silence...
Hey, what are you looking?
Blushing eyes drooped,
I summoned up courage to spill my heart bean,
Eh, I have got my dream.
With her sparkling eye shot flooded my empty heart with a feeling,
That ran through my whole being,
Ineffable feeling no word can define.
I still carry that pleasure in my heart,
Whenever I am out of mood,
Away from worldly rut,
I recollect that feeling,
Eyes of her still flashes...

Breaking my stupor,
Energetic I feel...
Oh, I have drunk nectar of her love divine.

Copyright Chandra Sekhar Batabyal
India

DIVINE ESSENCE

The outstanding treasure of life
To open the mystic heart
To shower rain of love
To touch the peak of paradise
Divine essence!
Love is blissful
Love is golden pool
Love is heavenly tub
Love spreads ray of life
Divine essence!
Love
Without any fear
Without any tear
The outstanding feeling dear
Divine essence!
Quest of mind
Beloved
Be a part of beautiful sky
When love makes the dreamy tower
Divine essence!
Live there with sweet dreams
Can reach the starry stream
So many colours so many butterflies
How beautiful this part
Divine essence!
Not need to mention
Only one issue
Pure essence of love
From the core of heart
Divine essence!
The Magic of love
Turns a bitter life into an adorable hut

Starts the new trend of life
The sweet dream of mystic life
Divine essence!
Love and love
Nothing can measure
Its magical mart
The beautiful aura of hidden art

Bangladesh

ONE LOVE CAN MAKE A PLEASURE

One love can makes me happy
My sense for goodness emotion
Makes to be so happy a lot
Since I deserve chance also
To be loved and stay loved
My endless sense for pleasured love
Must be settled for good zone
And I want to stay happy
I want to stay active also
My sense is on the good mood
I want to feel a taste
Which I never feel again
My world is also yours
And I seek emotions
To give only for you
My sense and my presence
I want to stay only goodness
I want to be just what I am
Pleasures of love is so gossip
When I give back to you
My world is also yours
Take me into the hand
And make me proud
Pleasured of your love
Intriguing my soul
I want to be so coolest guy ever
Even when I am so clumsy
To give my words a lot
But I always write love poems
Since you know that I love you.
I deserve to have a love
And you will surely understand

That love is gossip
Land of goodness zone
Even when we are far away!

I FEEL COMPLETE

I never knew how to love truly,
Since I met you everything changed totally,

Now I know how to surrender,
Believing nothing will put us asunder,

I have never before felt these emotions,
Being loved no matter the conditions,

Now I am addicted to your charms,
I always want to be in your arms,

I now look into my future without fear,
Because you wiped away my every tear,

I never believed love could be genuine,
With you I don't care if I go insane,

I don't care if loving you is a crime,
Because I no longer doubt this burning flame,

I love you with my soul and mind,
Every of your gesture has been kind,

In all ways you're rare,
You never hesitate to show that you care,

In my dreams I hear your voice,
I never regret that you're my favorite choice,

With I could serve a life time in jail,
Because we could.be happy together even in hell,

Ours together is a beautiful story,
I am counting the days before we marry,

With you I feel complete,
Inside my heart you have no substitute,

You have fulfilled my every wish,
What I feel for you is more than a crush,

Together our love is eternal,
Just by looking at your photos I go emotional.

I FEEL

What an amazing love!
I feel in my loneliness
I have never seen you
Till your love covers my life
Whenever you see my post

May be a writing, or a picture of a temple
You come and praise me
Your words are so lovely
That feels my heart with
Pleasure and joy
What a satisfaction it gives!

Cannot be described in words
I always search you in photographs,
In the kind hearted words,
It is nothing but pleasure of love
I do not know.

When we will meet someday
In the life.
Pleasure of Love is something
Seeing a garden full of roses
The sweet odour of colourful flowers
That fills my heart with joy

Pleasure of love
Is the sweet smile I see in your lips
The sweet words you speak to me
I always search your picture
That has sweet smiles

I love to hear your kind words
I love to see your sweet smiles
Which gives me happiness in my life.

Copyright Sharmistha Das

A POOL OF NO HURT

So I drank from this pool
Waters so pure,
Fumigated with love's tool.
Tastes of hates it cure,

It fertilizes a crumbling globe
Makes it full of health
Until grudges elope
To pave way for wealth.

Love does solve
Puzzles that chuckles
And overtly dissolve
Particles that entangles.

Love is a mirror
Reflecting not guilt
But projecting a hero
That imperfections built!

Can smiles embrace the face?
When imperfections stimulate?
Yet in love's pace
Comes joy at a crumbling gate!

O love, filled with gain,
So blind to hurt,
Erasing memories of pain
May men for you sought!

Mortals, drink from this pool,
Let satisfaction fill your womb!
With love as a stool,
God's clay live not in tomb!

Can earth suffer no more shame?
From inlets of segregation?
Can black and white the same,
Hugging in one congregation?

Come drink from this pool,
You, I, brothers be.
Love enrolls us in a school,
Guilt, it teaches not to see!

Come see unity in display!
Love has blinded my fault,
Now, peace comes to God's clay,
Sadness in sadly halt!

Love oh love,
Eraser of fault,
The binding curve,
Seasoning like salt!

A pool of no Hurt,
Come deepen your heart!
Here, the world knows no rot,
Brothers are all intact!

IF IT'S THE LAST THING I DO

Is it possible to love too much?
To love too hard.
Like a rage of affection
Corrupting my mind
Setting like cement in my heart
Forcing me to do anything necessary
Right or wrong
I am helpless
I am at your feet
Like a slave of absolute devotion
You have captured my soul
I don't want the key!
I don't want to be free!
Where would I go?!
What would I do?!
I only answer unto you
Crazy is an understatement
I am Infatuated, Obsessed,
Enchanted, Captivated,
Bewitched, Limerence,
Obligated to this feeling I yearn
This feeling of hope
This feeling of trust
This feeling of passion
This feeling of Love
I hear your unspoken words
I see your past
I see your hidden tears
I am your present
I want to be your future
The last thing I ever want to do
In my last breathing moments is;
Love you xo

UNWAVERING HAND

A prehensile part of the body.
made to handle.
another's child as one's own.
to pick up and hold with the unwavering hand.
as the child employs using his hands.
learning to walk.
to protect the child not to fall.
to have power or control over the child.
locking at each other's eyes.
smiling with each other.
enjoying the pleasures of love.
whilst walking together.
hand in hand.
follow love.
I met you and there was an instant connection.
from the moment we lock eyes.
you sense this in going to be different.
depending how madly in love you are with me.
the intensity of a man's chase.
to accept, to submit, to suffer.
to remain faithful.
to abide by your promise.
to embrace one's feelings.
this battle of love with me.
to await in expectation.
to catch.
the light of one's life.

PLEASURE OF LOVE

Mind soars in the firmament of lavish desires
Unfathomable the depth of happiness that fires
Unforgettable the moment when embraced
Within the arms of Love as if profoundly blessed.

In the garden of heart bloom the flowers of excitement
Bees and flies flutter round to play the game of amusement
Gentle breeze plays the guitar of mellifluous enchantment
Fortunate the owner of the garden having such nourishment.

The mute can yodel the hymns of loving melody
The blind can see the resplendent figure of fiancé
The deaf can hearken the amorous story afar
None is there who can't melt in the warmth of fire.

Love makes one the powerful emperor of the universe
Who can conquer the vast land of wonders tremendous?
Sowing the seeds of intoxication to fertile the brain stupendous
Like a drop of nectar enlivens life of slackness with no loss.

LOVE IS IMMORTAL

Every lover is mortal but love is immortal
No matter sweet or bitter, pleasant or fatal
Always spiral, spectacular, two ways communication in total
Like water turns from liquid to solid and solid to liquid.

Every ray of light be pale or dim but flicker of love sparkles
Day or night, rain or sun every situation tackles
However effects, affects or defects
Grows amidst the dense bushes of suspects.

Every life ends to let other live with sensibility
Life of love continues even after death in serenity
Man of serendipity can easily understand the value of love's agility
Possesses the sovereignty of gratitude and fortitude in dilemma or anxiety.

Love sings the songs of purity, clarity and integrity
Gives the slogans of equity, equality, justice and fraternity
Diverse shades germinate in diversity leading to unity
Sharing and caring in positivity can wash away the dirts of negativity.

MY DARLING SWEETHEART

Your love gives me pleasurable pleasure
So, I see you as my immeasurable treasure
My darling sweetheart,
Our love knows no season
Because, we have sundry reasons
To fall in love.
My darling sweetheart,
Your love gives me orgasmic pleasure
Which makes me see you as my treasure
Your love gives me new ray of hope
It makes me feel ti-ni-n-i
It makes me feel yori -yori
Your angelic kisses always echo "mwwee-mwee"
In my ears
Your sweet soft caresses earn me great pleasure
They make me un'stand the pleasure
Of love
They make me know the ecstasy of love
Your sweet soft caresses are as sweet as honey
They take me to unknown destinations.
My darling sweetheart,
When I look into your golden eyes
I see a bright
Future and I do rejoice
When I hear your silvery voice
I feel you're an angelic creature
With good hearted good nature
When I see your sweet smiles
They wipe away my tears and cries
Your hug is as warm as wool
And it gives me memorable pleasure
Which makes me yearn to spend more time with you

During our leisure.
My darling sweetheart,
Your love has given me a sense of adventure
Our love has taken us to beautiful scenes;
The Atlantic and the Mediterranean
The River Nile
The River Congo
The River Niger
The River Benue
We have flown across many mountains and hills
We have spent time both in the sun and in the rain
Even, our love has taken us to unknown destinations
This, proves that our love knows no season
My darling sweetheart,
With you, I have seen
And known the pleasure of love.

Nigeria

THERE IS PLEASURE IN LOVE

I'm very delighted to be loved
I have achieved love burning lots of woods
At first glance, the Night Queen is fully bloomed in mind
I was drowning in dreams at that night!

What were that diverse dream!
The next morning I was devastated like a night-bird
I collected the famous love quotes of poetry
And handed to her with trembling hands and she scolds me a lot!

I like her scolding, I like it a lot
And spent that night in a dream
The next day I was badly beaten
My ears are deaf to her scolding
The lover's abuse makes love stronger!

I was admitted to the hospital with this belief
She came on my discharge day from the hospital
The feeling of the day is indescribable!
How many things started to feel good
She caught me when I fell while walking
Lover's first touch above all comfort!

I floated in the air for three years
Traveling with a darling is very delightful
I wanted to touch her, I did
She never hindered or forbade

I used to enjoy lying on her lap with my eyes closed
Love after marriage carries a different flavor
Love between husband and wife is a kind of obligation
All happiness surpasses the joy of fatherhood
Grandpa's happiness is more than reaching on the
moon!

Love comes in many stages in human life
As a child, boy or adolescent, juvenile
In youth, maturity, finally old age
The pleasure of love at each stage is in a different mood
Pleasure rises in the sky, travels in the sea
Without love, there is no pleasure
Loveless pleasure is fiend
First learn to love own self, creatures, and then
environment
If there is true love, there will be pleasure.

SWEET LOVE IN THE WORLD OF FANTASY

Strolling along the serene lake, sad and lonely
Admiring breathtaking views around me
Cascading waterfalls flowing freely
Towering snow-capped mountain across the sea.

Oh! What a fantastic sight to behold!
Lovely multi-colored flowers growing wild
Their exquisite fragrance pervades in the air
While cool summer breeze caresses my hair.

Angelic nymphs are softly strumming their harps
Some are gracefully dancing to the tune of waltz
Cute hummingbirds are chirping merrily
Melodious tunes are in perfect harmony.

Soothing sweet music is played everywhere
Melodies I always love to hear
Consoles my weary heart and soul
My nostalgic heart is now in control.

Like magic, a man of great physique
Is standing humbly in front of me?
Wearing that mystic smile upon his lips
Was mesmerized for a moment and heart-stricken.

He bows and introduces himself to me
A noble prince from a kingdom far away
Perhaps he is the famous Adonis
Handsome lover of Greek Mythology.

Politely offers his hand for a dance
Feeling nervous, my hands are cold and numb
Singing and dancing all night long
In his loving arms is where I belong.

As hours go by, intense emotion grows
Whispering sweet words of love
Tenderly hugging, passionately kissing
Under the pale moonlight, one blissful night.

In love there is no barrier between lovers
Young and old, rich and poor
All is fair in love
To share the ecstasy of love.

Feeling sleepy and tired
Into his strong arms I retired
Resting my head upon his shoulder
Wherein, I feel safe to slumber.

When I woke up, my prince was not around
I searched and searched but nowhere to be found
Country music of Don William is in the air
I then realized, everything was just a dream.

Ah! What a wonderful dream it has been!
Wish to see you again my dear prince
In the next episode of my dream
In that colorful and marvelous realm!

NOSTALGIC HEART

Watching the magnificent sun go down
Lovely full moon awaits to claim her throne
To emit her ultimate splendor
For young and old to rejoice outdoor.

Noisy cicadas start roaming around
Cheerfully producing loud and shrill sound
Severe loneliness creeps into my soul
Yearning for loving arms to console.

Reminiscing sweet moment is heaven to me
No other love could ever comfort me
Only true love can make a memory
Misty-eyed, I look up to the sky and cry.

Never knew this strange feeling before
Your infectious smile made me love you more
Enticed me with your sweet and poetic tongue
Succumbed to your irresistible charm.

Only love can soothe my lonely heart
Only love can mend my broken heart
Only love can make my heart alive
Only heart can make my heart survive.

Where did I go wrong, left me sad and forlorn?
Spent some sleepless nights till break of dawn
All I need is your tender love
Come back to me my endless love.

What magic spell did you cast upon me?
Can't get you off my mind each night and day
If only I have a magic wand with me
To cast away this tremendous misery.

Hush! Hush! I hear a loud voice in the wind
Calm down foolish heart, be like a tamed gentle dove
For true love will surely finds its way
If it's meant to be to make you happy.

My prayer before I go to sleep at night
Lord, let him come to me in all his might
To take me away to the paradise of love
Showered with great from up above.

WHAT KIND OF LOVE

What kind of love is this from you to me
If I was told that there's love I'll always not agree
My life can testify even without opening my tools of speaking
I saw the flame of love and all my life received light
This is the sweetest feelings ever
Loving a woman that truly loves me is my biggest luck ever
My banana, my Rebecca let me stay with you forever
This feeling is like a drop of water into my oven
Your love is more than the world but like gaining the heaven
My heart always feel at ease that only you I face like figure seven
Right now I'm afraid if I were to choose between you and heaven believe it's over
My banana, my Rebecca let me be with you forever
Let me be by your side and run the race without falling back
This time that I sight you I fully know what peace really means so far
If I had known I would have come to thee since last year December
Have you seen the cutest ever?
Could you believe you're the best and the better
If I say I can trick down to heaven
Who want to dare me and I shall feed them with surprises by raven
Just let me hold one hand and see the magic
Let me hold her hand and see my strength and power and you'll be panicked

Let her profess me love and feel the real madness and my lunatic
For I might plough out a whole mountain of Everest
This feelings is different and I wish to live always in it
My heart desire, the cutest ever
Perhaps the world don't know two source of joy
One is to have God in you and feel loved by God
The other is to be loved by a woman that you love
Have you seen a man fighting against his destiny?
If heaven do not wish to give his blessings won't I fight?

A FEELING THAT CONNECTS HEARTS

Love is a feeling that connects hearts,
Revives to life, gives happiness,
Allows you to understand something deep and life-affirming.
Love is the pleasure of what we get
And from what we give.
The ability to experience pleasure
A necessary condition for
To fall in love with the right person.
Love relationships arise
When partners experience pleasure
From communicating with each other.
Love is a long and strong feeling of affection,
Implying sympathy for a person,
Desire to be near
Experience shared emotions
And also make each other happy.
You need to be attentive to the needs of a loved one,
Protect him and improve his quality of life.
People in love become close
Emotionally, physically, intellectually,
Sharing interests and tastes, combining habits.
Love colors our lives
The brightest colors.
Love can bring physical pleasure.
In the state of love we acquire the ability
See new opportunities there where they have not been seen before.
We are filled with a feeling of happiness.
We think our possibilities are endless.
That the world was made for two.
We are looking for a quiet, cozy place to be together.

We fall in love
That an ordinary person seems to us
The best in the world.
We make plans for the future
And gradually we are implementing plans.
We enjoy the fact that we met a person sent by fate.

Copyright Halyna Bokoch
Ukraine

LOVE BE 'THE THING

Baby love me as I love you
All will be pleasure on summertime.
Birds warbling joyful melodies,
Seagulls flying over the shore,
Waves breaking in the sea... rhythmical noise,
Yellowish Sun above in sky
to bask we under a little while...

Warmth of our hearts more than enough
to cuddle up tight affection.
The Love, we'll be growth itself growth.
We don't have to give up unto action,
true feeling of Youth forever.
Silence of old days... not aloofness...

Echoes of Love... heaven winners
Anyway... blind eyes will see us.
If a shadow comes as winter,
And we... lots of pain and rain...

Flooding Tears to treat us bad...
- We, gall wipe fast!
Born are we to Happy.
Crossing our way... nothing to hurt
We are meant to be forevermore affection...

In this world and after.
You and I, promise forever
Entwined hearts breathtaking Love.
Paradise... roses of a garden
That takes care to Mountains beauty of
Delicate and suave fragrance of petals...

Living short time... rose petals deny not Imbrication...
So does years of our romance...
Smelling good in a breeze of lust...
- We cast spell to other ones
Bewitched hearts... we taught how to love
For those whose feeling was unknown.

Copyright Maria Elvira Fernandes Correia

DIMENSIONS

Dunes reflect our Love kept, My Beloved
Decades rising, curving living movement
Wind carries memories infinite to
Find heart in warm light, find heart in cool shade

Seering Love light ignites inner fires
Flaring passions to loins entanglement
Wholly submitting in lovers embrace
Tide surges to climactic unison

Atop passions ridge our love suspended
Sea breeze whispers sweetness of arrival
New Love Divine a pleasure to behold
And so, the Dunes shift, twice over, twice blessed

Small thieves of sleep of time, reciprocate
With eyes filled with the sweetest purest self
Grains rise to windward as each new day dawns
With happiness and joy they find there place

Among the memories carried by Wind
Boldly they add dimensions to these hearts
Bubbly new spirits fly freely, we learn
Exuberance bursts from within giggling

Smiles shine through bedazzling all the senses
Glistening in our eyes how they have grown
Come trials together healing hands mend
Come sorrows, hearts true Love heals tenderly

Tears fallen settle peacefully leeward
The shifting sands dance upon Loves foundation
To see, to hear, to feel, to know, to be
In Loves multitude of rays that shine here

A life's blessings only ever dreamed of
With joyous pleasures many yet to come
This heart is thankful, this heart is humbled
My Beloved, this heart is only yours

Copyright Shamain Simeon
Aotearoa

IMMEASURABLE

Pleasure of love is undefined
It brings colours in life
Time ceases
Narcissists' plight.

Love paints biggest grim
Bestows faith within,
Losing oneself
In owns' sight.

In velvety night
Akin midnight moon
Intertwined
For rest of lives.

Magic of love
Stars in eyes
I can hear my heart rush
In wanderlust soul.

A beautiful madness
Always on cloud nine
I breathe in melody
Sway with tides

Colours of spring
Lingers on my tongue
Sunshine and rain
A world of magic

Pleasure of love
Metamorphosis
Of soul
Can't trade for anything in the world.

Copyright Anjana Prasad
India

I LONG

I long to nestle in HIS love
As stars and moon
In azure sky vast
Serene and profound.
Unlimited, unfathomable
More than life.

Let His light guide
My path
In the darkest night
Faith and fate
Embellished
In HIS love.

Today and forever
HIS smiles wipe my despair
I on the path of glory
Hum a new story
For I long for heaven
In this life.

Beyond is unknown
Realms of paradise
Unexplored.
Unaware of rebirth
And incarnations
Disguised.

Beyond the shadows
Until the day breaks
God is light
God is love
The last truth
Triumph o'er life

India

LOVE IS A UNIQUE EXPERIENCE

Love can't be defined,
It can only be experienced.
For some it is a pleasure,
For others it may be pain,
What is it exactly?
No one can explain!

Let us explore it,
Dive deep inside,
As we plunge deeper,
It appears even brighter,
A journey into the light!

Those who tried it earlier,
Couldn't fathom its depth,
All they could say,
Was a wonderful experience?
Blissful anyway!

The observer and the observance,
Become really one,
The wall between collapses,
Differences, distinctions none!

Both identify with each other,
In all most all respects,
At this stage, there is no desire,
Further demands or protest.

One feels voluntarily ready
To suffer any pain, sacrifice anything,
Share everything, hide nothing,
Devotion, dedication, submission,
The bond becomes liberation!

No carnal desires, only a spiritual fire,
Keeps burning, thoughts churning,
Love, pure as gold, emerges shining.
Pleasure of love can't be measured,
By what you gain always,
But how much you are willing
To suffer and sacrifice,
He is a true lover,
Who is pleased to pay the price?

India

EVERY TIME I THINK ABOUT YOU

Every night I see you in my dreams
Every night I feel your presence
Though you are from afar
Every day I think about you
Cos your love gives me pleasure
Every day I think about you
And the thought of you being my wife
Flows in my brain regularly;
As regular as the clock so I think about you.
From the first time I set my eyes on you
I prayed that God should allow me marry you
That day I first met you, I believed I've come to my final
Bus-stop
That day I first set my eyes on you
I believed I've found my rightful rib
My darling angel, from the first moment I met you
I was completely smitten by you
My darling Angel, every time I look into your eagle eyes
I'm fully convinced that I've found a lovable love
Every time I see you walk
I see the African queen of the twenty first century.
My darling Angel, I long to hear
Your angelic sweet voice with a silver tone
For it gives me pleasure
I wish to feel your protective and warm body
For your body is as warm as wool
So, I wish you should give me a hug
Cos, in your warm arms
I feel like Lazarus in heavenly places.
My darling Angel, my heart is yours;
You do not need a visa before you intrude into my heart
I've opened my heart for you

So, please, open yours for me too
For I'm waiting patiently to enter
Please, keep the door ajar
I promise, I shall never disappoint you
You will be the only one in the paradise of my heart
In fact, my heart will be your humble abode forever!

Copyright Asua Tyongi Gabriel
Nigeria

LOVE IS WILLING TO SACRIFICE

Thank you for the love you share
We always spend the time together
Building the castle of love we care
Filling gladness in the life forever
I will do everything
Making our love meaningful
As the pleasure of love we bring
Changing our world so wonderful
Happiness is simple way
Having peace heart and joyful life
Overcoming temptation right away
Living to enjoy life so safe
Our love is bright sunshine
Brightening the world so true
When we just see the rain
And no one knows when we feel blue
Love never feels doubt
Giving the light of happiness
Love always offers the wings of hope
Softening yearning with tenderness
I pray to ask God
Matching us in unity
As the pleasure of love is so good
We are not afraid to face the reality
I will be willing to die
Fulfilling the pleasure of love we find
Love never cheats or tells lie
Love shows honesty so fine
I'm sorry if I hurt your feeling
Love always thanks for God's blessing.

TO WHOM MY EYES PRIES FOR

In my Palace exists a Queen
She's born and crowned
She's vested with the things
Things supposed for the throne
She save sinking souls
If it were in those days
She would have been named soul
For she fought wars
I wish I should be your Prince
Atleast if not king
But since I won't have a vice
I shall spread my wings
I would boast for an increased fit
For I will be enjoying the feast
Please never mind my errors
Lest I die in horror
Hold my hand
Let them play the bands
As we showcased
Our love to the face of the whole universe.
Let's create jealousy
As we trample into the wishes of evil hearts
And sign our license of love
Whine the curves of the heap
Into the skies we win
Win the competition feasted for lover birds
For the fare of my heart flight you have paid
Race me around the rooms of pleasures
Let's dance to the rhymes
Vibes played for our darling love
Never leave this path of our love
Till we reach it destination.

MAGIKAL LOVE

Love whispers face to face.
The heart seeks the other heart.
In your eyes my dreams are read,
Which I whisper to you with a heart in love.
It is a pleasure of love is mutual.
A world - filled with dreams,
In which I and You are we.
Magical love - It makes people good!
Love whispers face to face.
The heart seeks the other heart.
Soul to soul - gently whispers
Love is we -
Me and You!

Copyright Silviya Veselinova
Bulgaria

SUCKER FOR LOVE

Everybody sucks in love.
The greatest weakness of all time, breaking the strongest of humans whether young or older.
No one is too strong when it comes to the above.

Muscles won't help you, experience won't either,
No matter how strong you are you will fall and rise and fall again even harder when it comes to love.
We take baby-steps and fall down but we still keep trying harder.

Some call it lust but I ask which is more potent, lust or love?
I make bold to say its love not lust that made Adam take the fruit from Eve to in order to please her.
It is love not lust that makes us act a fool, manhandled, fight like cats and still resolve.

It is love not lust that made God to trust man even when he knew man will fail him.
Love can be greedy like a raven and yet luring many to her trap with the face of a dove.
Love is blind yet we walk into it with our eyes wild open never wanting to stay off.
Even the Thug-Life crooner confessed to this weakness so am standing on a giant shoulder.

We act tough but on the inside we are babies still trying to figure out this thing call love.
We stay striving to win hearts that has long been taken by another.

Can one really own someone else's heart without being given on the bases of true love?
Am a sucker for love so even though our love sucks I rather be with you than with another?

Love deferred makes the heart ponder so please darling don't take me off.
Give me your love cause it's stronger than any element even ether.

Copyright Jackson Agocha
Nigeria

EVER SINCE WE RANG

Ever since we rang
Everyday has been one
Too close to be apart
Our hands have been warm
You show me colours of your heart
And there is still more to see
I taste every part of you
And there is still more to taste
Glad we met
Despite the many around
There is no way it is a coincidence
The winds are always in motion
The seas are rough
Even the fishes are moved
So this is fate
Written before we met
You feel the air
With an atomic nostalgia
Always calling me
I need another sniff
You praise me well
Even when I'm wrong
You know the right words
When I'm down
We've had our share
Of broken glass
Hurting our feet
Almost a cancer, but we prevailed
None is perfect
And that's fallen on us
Stones have been thrown
And we've healed the wounds

Tears have fallen
Sometimes unwiped
A sorry has been said
Sometimes not taken

Broken we've been
Sometimes far apart
But our hearts have found ways to hold
Keeping us together
Glad we met
Despite the many around
There is no way it is a coincidence
The winds are always in motion
A roller-coaster we've ridden
Sometimes scary
Sometimes lovely
Sometimes through the tunnel
But always our hands we've held.

LION CUB

Mother Mother
A lioness stutter
From where i came
To where i hover
In your mouth
I've called my home
Your teeth never bit
Like life is not a comb
With you i walked
When hunting was the hub
Sometimes alone i was
For safety, i would pause
And in feast we would claws
Father Father
A lion stutter
From where i came
To where i hover
With your mane i play
A crown you would one day lay
With you i walked
When the pride was flawed
As another tested
And you pound and roared
Forcing him out
Saving me from his count
A lesson i vowed
In the wild
I am applied
Out of the pride
A threat i was
My claws out of my paws
Pealed eyes

Any threat must be clawed
Open ears
Every sound must be stored
Alone i am,
Time for a roar
Mother mother thanks for the love
Father father thanks for the work
I guess it's time to be a lion like you all

LITTLE ONE, LITTLE ONE

Who comes to this Earth
With Smiles on its face
And Smiles on ours too
Little one, little one
With a heart full of joy
A glow that never goes
A hand full of life
Little one, little one
With innocent looking eyes
Catching all our rays
And nothing to reflect
Little one, little one
With dirt on its skin
Cries sound the air
You fell on the ground
Little one, little one
You know not of none
Your skin, soft as snow
You melt in my hands
Little one, little one
Your frown makes me cry
Just laugh for me once
You know not of none
Little one, little one
You come to this world
Steal all our hearts
And grow out of us
Little one, little one
The world waited you
You troubled all our heart
And made us worry-aid
Little one, little one

The smoke of this world
Runs deeper than looks
I hope not in your eyes
Little one, little one
Days come and go
It waits not for none
You better live it well
Little one, little one
Like I change you up
I want you clean always
Whenever you get stained
Little one, little one
Drink not of the milk
That flow in malice dam
It might just make you sick
Railway Gray

LOVE'S PLEASURE

I saw a pair of albatrosses
Roaming over the blue sky
Waves below danced merrily
I imagined the pleasure of love.

I saw a pair of dolphins
Jumping and diving in blue sea
Cool breeze blew gently
I imagined the pleasure of love.

A saw a pair of swans
Swimming in a lotus pond
Sun smiled in morning calm
I imagined the pleasure of love.

I saw a pair of sparrows
Chirping on a thatched roof
Dew drops sparkled below
I imagined the pleasure of love.

I saw a pair of squirrels
Chasing each other on a tree
Leaves rustled with wind
I imagined the pleasure of love.

I saw a pair of serpents
Curling like long twisted hair
Green hedges stretched longer
I imagined the pleasure of love.

A saw a pair of butterflies
Playing hide and seek in bush
Golden rays warmed the grass
I imagined the pleasure of love.

I saw a pair of flowers
Kissing each other gently
Zephyr helped them come closer
I imagined the pleasure of love.

I saw a pair of rocks nearby
Calling us to come nearer
We sat there hand in hand
I felt the pleasure of love.

THE POWER OF LOVE

Love is more powerful,
It is unconditional,
It is a precious gift,
It is beyond lust,
It only sees the beauty of heart and soul,
It gives light when you are in the dark,
It gives shade when you are in the sun,
It heals you when you are wounded from within,
It gives you support when you need it,
It is a symphony that fills you with eternal bliss.
It touches your soul by going through the heart,
It sparkles into your eyes and gives you priceless happiness,
It is a pure feeling that makes you a good person,
It touches you deeply and teaches you to live for someone,
It teaches you to care about someone, for whom your heart beats faster,
It gives you the vision due to which you find only the goodness in someone,
It teaches you to pray for someone's wellbeing,
It makes your deserted life happy,
It gives you a reason to smile again,
It gives you immense pleasure and the treasure of life.
Love is divine,
It makes you feel high,
It takes you on a journey to heaven,
It gives you beautiful dreams even during the day,
It is a magic potion that soothes your heart,
It is the elixir of life that gives peace to your soul,
It is a pleasant rain in which you feel infinite joy by getting wet,

It creates a positive energy inside you,
It gives you the strength to fight every storm,
It is a magical feeling that can't be described in words.\

Copyright Deepti Shakya
India

THE PLEASURE LOVE BRINGS

Every life that moves on land
Even the seas, the desert sands
All do bleed, the color red
And all feel love, in their heart and head

Love can touch the weakest of hearts
Or the strongest, who won't let, emotions impart
Travelling across the mountains and seas
An emotion that follows no rules or boundaries

Animals, birds, just like human beings
Do feel love, and the pleasure it brings
Love makes the heart feel ardent and light
Floating on air, like a bird taking flight

The pleasures of love can be felt by all
Who learn to live for other's sake?
For, love is meant to be, given before
Someone's love, you willingly take

Caring, for that person, you really love
Brings pleasure, to see them smile
Loving them the way they want to be loved
For, each one seeks love, in their own style

You need to give love, to find love can be
So pleasurable, that you can't, let it go
And as each day goes by, that love multiplies
New pleasures to relish, you get to know

Love can be of different kinds
And so does the pleasure it brings
Love for a friend, a lover, a pet
Dear family, or your siblings

Love for your country, your motherland
Ahead of all love, this love stands
Love for your music, a game, or a phone
Every love gives us pleasure of its own

The pleasure and joy from each love may differ
But they all do satisfy our heart
And stay with us forever, as memories to hold
Until from this world we depart

So in the end I'll say, that if from love you're at bay
Then try n find, what's keeping it away
'Cause, however deep or shallow it may sound, you need to feel love around
To feel the pleasures, only found in love's way...

EYES

Time has passed by
Feelings are thrown away
Wet memories
We seek salvation for ourselves
Your eyes are glowing weirdly
What was u tryna tell me
The magic does not stop
The glow of heaven in a candle.
The lightning strikes a flare
In the eyes of the azure color

Not even a hope will play
Quenching the discord.
The sea in Zenice
I'm overwhelmed by the grace
The smile on the lips
In the soul there is an unusual tide.
A view of the deep ocean
Stuck in your eyes
You are my magical dream
A challenge to a cruel fate.

Copyright Duška Kontić
Montenegro

THE GLOW OF THE SKY

It still hurts that one
An unseen brilliance
Of to the unknown
The hiding place of souls
Let me come to you
I would like to...

When you least expect it...
On this sunny autumn
Let me paint for you
With my fingers in the eyes
From the leaves of the multicolored
Let me make you
May you be the most beautiful to me
How are you doing?

Why have you gilded the heavens
It smelled like weed
Laying down from sadness
The nights of the rainbow
They don't take it apart
Thunder and lightning
Of the heavens
The verse fell asleep
In the core of my thighs
Dedicated to you!

Copyright Duška Kontić
Montenegro

BECAUSE I LOVE YOU...

Because I love you
I have placed a photo of us
Not only on the study table
Where I sit and write

I have imprinted it in my heart
Because I love you
The ditties we sung together
Are not only recorded in gramophone

They are my lifelines
I hum them all the times
Because I love you
Constant gazing into your irises

Never tires me
It rather infuses life in me
As I read your unpronounced love for me
Because I love you
Your embraces aren't enough
To be entwined in you
My soul and spirit
Yearns for communion beyond this earthly love!

BEAUTY OF LOVE

He looked into her beautiful eyes
Deer like and got captivated in them
Embraced her in his arms
Aww! Both drenched in warmth bounteous

Unmindful of shy glances of onlookers
They swirled in the breeze of emotions benign
Bathed in the waters of surging swirling ocean
Hues of love dipped in the paint of vivacious vibrance

He kissed her forehead in mirth and joy
Waves and ripples locked in passionate kiss
Flame of love burned like a pious fire
Intense love intertwined heart's yearnings

A rapturous symphony filled air with love tender
Stars and moon blessed the lovers from above
Behold! Beauty of love! how Lovers hold each other's heart tightly
Lost in the depth of emotions they make a new start.

Copyright Ritu kamra kumar

LOVE IS NOT ENOUGH

Sensual friendships in youth
the bewitching portrayal of love
In fiction and movies elevate love
To the pedestal of romance and trance

Love is not only about promises
Of Jocund joys untold
Oscillates it between trivial tiffs
Honest hilarious moments manifold

Aww! Love is not enough to nurture relationships
A commitment it is between two souls
To revel in reveries
Sharing miseries is always needed

The charm, curiosity and congeniality
Of blissful bonds withstands adversity
The lustrous hair fall, mesmerizing eyes bespectacled
Lover's affinity transcends all fatalities

Bathed in the holy waters of care, compassion
Pledges and promises spiritual unions take place
Emotional connect and empathy moors love to secure
harbor in grace
Where each day it springs

And illuminates like summer
Ecstasy like heavenly showers
Life becomes a metaphor loved with Divine Luster

THE DIVINE JOY

Material things can't bring
Happiness as nature does
Everything's available
For free in this universe

Colourful blooms, butterflies
Chirping birds and fragrant breeze
Glorious dawn's shining rays
Filtering through the dense trees

Wandering clouds, in the sky,
Playing hide and seek with sun
Create beautiful rainbow
That is a sight full of fun

Flying skylarks and sparrows
Are feast for onlookers' eyes
Swimming ducks in the water
Give my aesthetics a rise

Undulating waves of sea
And drifting boats with white sails
It's a mesmerizing view
Whose magic spell never fails?

I adore all these beauties
Love the idea of love
Dreaming of a charming prince
Give myself a pleasant bluff

Ecstasy of attachment
Is out of the world, I feel
Let love permeate the earth
I hope, wish, pray and appeal

It's hypnotic and unique,
Inexplicable pleasure
Do not abandon love, folks!
It's the ultimate treasure

Copyright Sudha Dixit

LETTERS UNSENT

I have a whole lot of unsent letters
All addressed to you and only you
In all miss not the word with three letters
Of the feeling that has always felt new.

Yes, the letters are unsent
With words in them well penned
Words to you I've wished to tell
Only that they were impossible to spell.

Letters with memories of your eyes, blue
Memories from the time I stole glances at you
By the corner of my eye
To now: imagining us walking down the aisle.

At times I plan to sent one or two
Or even bring them by hand to you
And watch you read them
Thou all the words in them are same.

LOVE IS ALL THAT MATTERS

Love makes any moment so precious
It defines a moment in time
Like a rare gem, treasured
Kept for a lifetime

Love puts me in a world so strange
Everything around me changed
Full of beautiful dreams
Happiness that makes a heart sing

When I am with you
I feel my dreams come true
We traveled far on our way
Found good and bad things to say

How I love what you do for me
No detail is so small
Because of love you do it all
Here you stay deep in my heart and soul

I'm so precious in your sight
I see it in your approving eyes
In my darkest hour
You are my light

A loving heart finds joy in sentiments
Weaves song out of tears
Brings music in silence
Turns sorrow into poem

Tenderness in pain
Behind all joys and tears
All the years spent together
The times we almost fall

What counts most of all
Is, how well we love each other
'Cause love is all that matters

Copyright Ulma Taboada

AND THE GREATEST OF THEM ALL IS LOVE.

No greater philosophy can ever outwit the wisdom of love.
No greater religion ever existed but the religion of Love.
No greater belief has ever been proven tacit than love.
No greater doctrine can ever replace the precepts of love.
No greater commission was given to mankind but to love God and man.
No greater duty is nobler for man to do but to love his neighbor.
No greater education can be taught than the experience of loving.
No greater extreme challenge exist than loving those who hurt and hate you.
No greater security can ever be reliable than being surrounded by love.
No greater economic crisis could bring to poverty a loving person.
No greater joy can ever be felt than the result of loving the unlovable.
No greater hope one could cherish than finding out somebody loves you.
No greater experience can one have but to love and be loved.
No greater technology can ever teach the manners Love.
No greater opportunity one could grab than the elusive moment to love.
No greater reward could match any grand prize than the consolation of love.
No greater sin is ever unpardonable by a merciful and forgiving Love.

No greater dream anybody ever aspire than to be truly loved.
No greater punishment is effective to any stubbornness but a firm love.
No greater psychological treatment could ever relieve the mind but Love.
No greater ugliness exist when viewed through the mirror of love.
No greater heroic deed can ever surpass the simple acts of love.
No greater cold apathy can ever divide us from the warmth of love.
No greater distance can ever be far that love could not reach.
No greater heights is ever too high that love could not touch.
No greater government is ever stable than the one whose foundation is love.
No greater nation can ever be stronger than a people who love each other.
No greater wealth of the entire world combined can ever buy a priceless Love.
No greater death is ever sweet than to die in the name of Love.
No greater language can ever been universal than the language of love.
No greater force can ever be stronger than the strength of love.
No greater war is ever fought than the battle of Love against sin and hate.
No greater evil is ever wicked that was not defeated by the power of Love.
No greater deity that has ever existed than the God that is Love

No greater of all the greatest in the whole universe but Love.
Yes and the greatest of all is LOVE.

Copyright Marvin Marcelino

THE CHOSEN VESSEL

Love delights the human soul
Igniting a feeling to behold.
Like a music lyre of passionate glow
Played on a perfect day to an emotion grows
Kindling the fire to power your side
As though a melodic string desires your oars in all its strides.

As sweeter than honey,
It restores the soul.
Emulsifiers all its tastes as comely,
It heels bestows in purity of gold.
Conforming minds at last to yearn to stupor
What pleasant souls makes hay for succor.

Love leads the way to the heart
It renders a key that paves a path
And keeps fond memories to linger for all times
In a heart of heart that bears a gold mine
Erupting joyous derivatives of feelings to go by and bye
Happy feelings that sways like an air that sighs.

Copyright Ivina Emmanuel Asoh

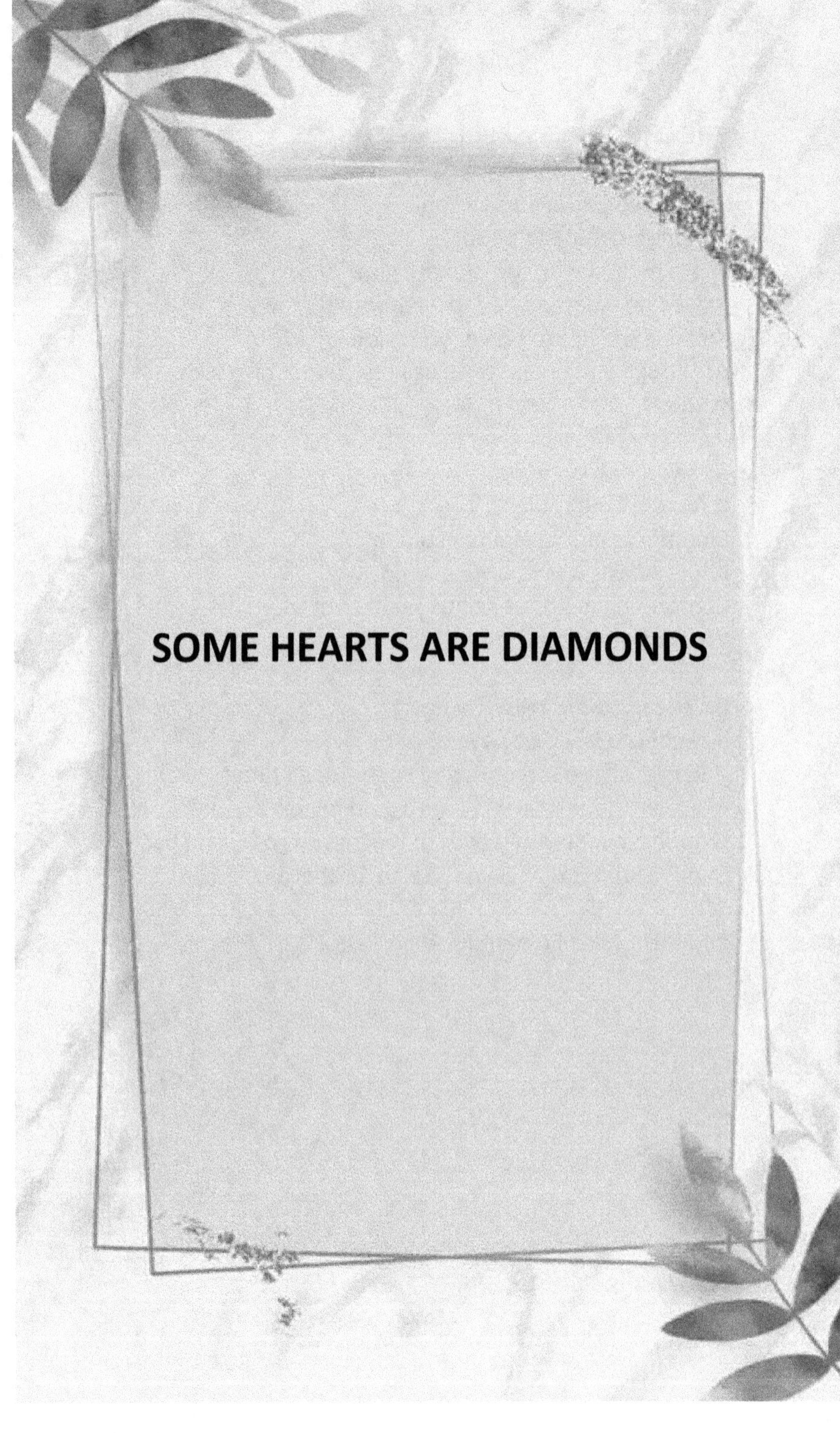

SOME HEARTS ARE DIAMONDS

DESPITE OLD SCAR

When you are loved
You become a star
A precious diamond
Despite your old scar.

You are so much needed
That you are a reason
And a cause for existence
In each and every season.

For sure you are real
A reason for caring
You are my excellent calm
In a season of daring.

A brilliant star you are
No one can mar
A joy to behold
Much rarer the gold

When you are loved
You become a star
A precious diamond
Despite your old scar.

Copyright Loreta C Bande
Philippines

DISA ZEMERA JANE DIAMANTE

Mbi floket tane gjethet binin
dhe ere e lehte sa me s,kish
dhe dielli kuqerremte humbiste
tej hapesires ne perendim.
Nuk duhej dita te mbaronte
as perendim s,duhej te kish.
Mbi floket tane ere vjeshtes
dic mermerinte fshehtesisht.
Ne perendim te asaj dite
qe ikte ne rrugen pa kthim,
ne hapsire dic regetinte
si diamant zemera jote ne mos harrim.

Copyright Ollga Farmacistja
Albania

RESIDUAL ROMANCE

Love changes
Impossible to foresee
Evolves or dissolves
Only guarantee
Our youthful dreams
Did not reach fruition
Casualties of Fate
Her intervention
Disappointment
Damaged your spirit
Heart once aglow
Lost sparkle within it
Will you allow
Another chance?
Try once more?
Polish residual romance?

HEARTS ARE DIAMONDS

Into my sense
And my presence
Heartbeats shows
For my many ways
To stay so happy
Some hearts are diamonds
If you choose happiness
I will stay happy
My sense and my way
I will stay so good
Hearts are my way
To stay so goodness
My love and my all
I wish to stay amazing
My time and my world
Will be settled forever
Hearts are diamonds
World seeks me also
My sense also needs
Some good sense.

Copyright Amb Maid Čorbić

WHOSE HEART IS THAT

Full of joy
Like a vivid diamond glow
They say diamonds are forever
I sure hope that's true
That heart keeps on thumping
As long, as it can excel
Which beats and breathes
Life in a hearty asylum
Of blessed piety
Of great devoutness
And jeweled purity
Together with everything in formation
Like a diamond shining
With illustrative
Silhouette carvings

WHEN I COULD NOT FIND YOU

When I could not find you on my shore
When my feet failed to drive me to your door
When I want to touch the strings
With care, I cover your fluttering wings
With a song saying that we shall start
And save a wrinkling fading heart
Make it wear robes of pearls
Because when pearls in a heart shine
All the lanes smile and everything is fine
I want to get up and badge
The pebbles, growing into a stone
Blocking rivers of passion and glee
Wiping off all the rage, because I do know
Hearts that tasted love do bow
To the hymns of a truthful love vow
Just let's come with me and tread
That rosy lanes whereupon
You sing your melody and read my poetry

LISTEN TO TALES OF HEARTS

Listen to my heart as you know
I am telling a tale of some beautiful hearts
That are more valuable like diamonds
That are hearts most precious

That are hearts that keep love
That are hearts that never treat bad
That are hearts that keep promises
That are hearts which soothes the soul

That are hearts that heals others
That are hearts who rules the hearts
That are hearts that make others happy
That are hearts that win others hearts by love

Listen to my tale of those hearts
That hearts are diamonds
That hearts spread fragrance
That hearts are beautiful

That hearts worshipped only God
Listen to my tale of beautiful hearts
Listen to the voice of those hearts in pain
May those hearts live long

May those hearts never fail nor fall
May those hearts keep their flow
May I achieve the grace of those hearts
May my heart be the fellow of those beautiful hearts

May my heart be shine like diamonds
May my love for humanity has no bounds
May my heart be shine like sun
May my heart and soul are in one way

RAREST DIAMOND

Darling, you always lived in my heart
Your being so near, inevitable
Coz you are so very precious
I loved having you in me

My most cherished secret
A secret I kept from the world
They never could understand my smiles
It was your sense of humor

They never could fathom my twinkling eyes
It was your unconditional love
They never could know about my skin glow
It was your soul caressing touch

My face radiating your love
My soul shining brightest than the sun
My being emanating serenity
The purest form of love I received from you

It touched the core of my being
A rarest of rare diamond was your heart
Rarest of rare diamond
Rarest of rare diamond

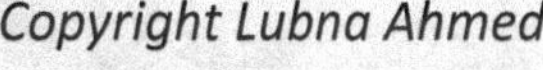

SPEAK OUT

Speak out, my love ,
Why you shed tears in silence,
Your tears glisten with beads of fallen dreams,
I can't allow your dreams to die.

I love you,
And for your smile to bloom,
I can do everything for you.
You love me too, I know,
You can share me your woes.

I can pierce,
You possess a loving heart,
That's enough to me,
To wipe out your tears and glow your face smiling,

We both will weave new dreams,
And forget all the past pains.
I seems a new dawn ushering,
After the night's bad dreams fading.

Copyright Chandra Sekhar Batabyal
India.

DIAMONDS....

Reflecting light as it dances in the darkest night...
Easiest to steal but hardest to break...
Yet our hearts are not as strong as diamonds...
For it's fragile as glass and even with the softest of touch it can crack...

Moving forward and never looking back...
Afraid to stop as your body may follow the order...
Your spirit may keep going beyond the border...
Woah is your fragile heart...

Reflecting what it wants but can never have...
Realizing you are on your own and always have been...
Growing smarter in moments day by day...
Yet becoming older and more foolish with your heart...

Building the walls and the ice to make it cold...
Being your own savior...
Soon it becomes labor....
Routing for yourself when no one else will...

Injustice but like diamonds glimmer so bright....
Untruths bejeweled as your heart dies...
Losing hope in a download slope...
Yet we must shine our light from within...

We are not diamonds...
Neither is our heart...
We are true illuminations to be shared as an art...
Share your song...

Be the truth...
Note to self...
Just be you...

Copyright Tha Ono

YOU'RE PRECIOUS

I look back with pride,
In spite of everything our love didn't fade,

I am glad you didn't quit,
On trust our love was built,

We fell and rose to our feet,
We were the talk in every street,

In my heart you're precious,
All the others are just jealous,

I never let you know your worth,
I love you more than anything else on earth,

Your presence has no price,
I want to be seen with you in every place,

We are perfectly matched in heaven,
Without you I would be frozen,

Baby with you I would never surrender,
I see angels when we kiss so sweet and tender,

I am happy you believed,
I know its how we survived,
When you smile I see rainbow colours,
You know how to satisfy my desires,
Baby you're my wings of freedom,
I need you with every cell of my system.

GOLDEN HEART STILL EXISTS!

You don't know
The meaning of love?
True love comes
From Golden heart.

It needs to search
To see to sketch
Your dreamy arts
Searching dear Golden heart.

Don't worry dear
Though you hear
Some painful words
From Unfathomable heart.

That's also fine
Never mind
Still there's the golden heart
It will love till the death.

This must be bloomed
Within all hearts
Not need to feel so sad
Though Golden heart can't hold so easily.

SEEKING LOVE

Songs of love drift
With the winds of change
Sleepless nights spent once
To tend the ephemeral
Turn to stories of yore strange.

Broken chords jar
To create music of discord
Two faces turned to two walls
Nurse blank stares in cold hearts
Consuming a room, once a citadel of love- lord!

Closed chapters whimper on closed windows
No breath of fresh recourse
Opens up sealed hearts
The butterfly of rainbow bright
Bangs and flutters to death unsung in remorse.

Some hearts are cold
That smell of tombstones
My restless wings fly
To reach and embrace
The hearts of molten gold!

A HEART OF A DIAMOND

The first day I saw you were a precious jewel to me.
I could hear it in your voice, and your Royalty I could see.
Diamonds have a very special place in my heart.
The melody I am hearing, is come here, sweetheart.

You have a heart of a Diamond, you are my true turtle dove
A rare precious blend, kind of heavenly love.
It's not earthly natural, it truly comes from above.
Your heart is a Diamond that sings like an Angelic choir is pure Godly love.

Heart of a diamond that's what you are to me.
Heart of a diamond that's what you are to me.
When I hear your precious heartbeat, I hear music to my ears.
I can't believe that I am listening to music of the spheres.

Dominance has taken over, my heart wants, what it wants.
Having heard your heartbeat makes me just want to flaunt.
Flaunt the love that is so obviously in my heart.
Knowing that it glitters like a Diamond from the very start.

You are the heart shaped diamond that Cupid aimed towards me.
My heart is so very happy, we are having a jubilee.
Heart of a diamond that's what you are to me
Heart of a diamond that's what you are to me
Heart of a diamond that's what you are to me
Heart of a diamond that's what you are to me

Copyright Marion Remnant Parish

SUNNY FAIRY TALE

The sound of piano is heard by the seaside
A woman's hand on the shoulder of a player
Her eyes shine, the music touches the heart
He found suddenly in the valley of tears.

The waves are whispering, they tell a story
On the waterfront a man and a beloved woman
As the hours slowly ticking away
Tremble in love with no time.

They sit like that, it's in their hair
Maybe they've been looking for each other for years
They are not found in young dews
Forgetting what they dreamed long ago.

A quiet fire going on in the fireplace
Arms folded, the calm of the day
Spotted in the clear moonlight
Two souls, like one to dream.

The moon slowly over the house
A woman seen in his eyes
Only he knows the harsh truth
Of perplexed roofs on a deserted night.

Copyright Duška Kontić
Montenegro

BOLD HEARTS

Bold heart's tales are told after they're held by earth untold
You are what you like
You are what you seek
You are what you speak
You are what you think
Think of making a heart of glass
Glass that reflects your heart classy
Classy you can identify hearts messy
Messy hearts can make nothing worthy
Worthy hearts dare not make anything clumsy
Clumsy hearts care none but self like a Prince
Princy are hearts very rare
Goldy are hearts very rare
Get not dejected or be scared
You can still make a word beautiful for you
You can still create smile beautiful for you
Aim of being a childlike heart ever
Train yourself to be selfless ever!
You can make a a world lovable
You can still remain a soul simple
Get not influenced by mean people
Get not manipulated by evil thoughts!
Let your heart be pure
Let you be everyone's cure

LOVE IS WHAT WE NEED

Love is what you look for in life
But trust is what, makes you think, still twice
Sometimes it's just you, who loves them utmost
But their kind of love is, 'keep changing the host'

Years go by, and there they are
Coming back again, like a newly painted car
With hearts that show love, but not true at all
'Cause diamonds don't break, like glass, when they fall

Tears roll down, when each time you're hurt
You think it's the last, won't fall for such flirts
But then loneliness, leaves your throat dry
Making you hope, this one seems right, so let's try

But not every heart is the stone you deserve
A precious diamond, in your heart to preserve
A counterfeit stone, can be set on a ring
But only true hearts, when joined, true love they bring

I've waited for you, all through these years
Hoping someday, I'll get to wipe all your tears
My love for you now, is same as before
But what's in your heart, I'd sure like to know

For, love is what we both need
And trust me when I say, I'm a diamond indeed
This time your trust, won't end up in pain
'Cause I won't let your heart, break ever again

TRUE HEART IS DIAMOND

Whilst we are together
I try to seek smiles
Hope in agony
You gaze lonely streets

As hard as a diamond
We always loved to watch the sky
Had our own perceptions
I loved the horizon

Where the sky meets the earth
You tried to fathom vastness.
Which has more beauty
Sunrise or sunset?

No matter what
Every heart that breathes love
Is happiest like a diamond rare
When the heart plays

A tuneful melody
Emanates love akin to the
Radiance of a diamond.
The magic of happiness and true love

DON'T DESPAIR MY LOVE!

I know you have been badly hurt
By your true love unrequited
I know you're still licking the wounds
You got from false promise cited

I know that you've lost faith in love
But trust me that love does exist
Not everyone is stone hearted
Do not let pessimism persist

The universe is full of love
A most natural element
One wrong step or bad occurrence
Should not leave scar that's permanent

Each one of us is entitled
To obtain our quota of love
To look after us we have there
Our guardian angel above

All hearts are not akin to stones
Some like diamonds are real gems
Wait for pure love with faith and hope
Envision joy minus problems

Copyright Sudha Dixit

TREASURES IN THE BODY

Science we study
Archeology we practice
Mineralogy we learn
Mining we perform

All in search of resources
Hidden beneath the earth
But who mines the heart?
Silver and gold we seek

For platinum and diamonds
We hustle and struggle
Toiling day and night
For them to acquire and keep

But who seek the heart?
Jewelries are good
And how pleasing they are
To the one that've got them

And more so are they
When they're of precious stones.
Yet better lies within us.
Children are cute and lovely

And they joy of a home
Desiring are they
Upon the families wish list
Taking the center stage.

But more so
And above all
Is the joy and happiness
From a pure and beautiful soul

Reflecting affection
Than the lights of a diamond
Blessed is the world by the universe
Who deposited such treasure within us?

And till my eyelids to the sun close
Yours will I hold with me so
For now I know
That treasures purer and more precious

Than ornaments of silver,
Gold, platinum or diamond
Lie not only in the soil
But in bodies likes yours.

GOLD AND ROCK

I have been dwarfed by your moon's shine
How can I touch your chin?
I have been drawn to gaze at you
To excavate your mind's texture.

I was startled to know that you are a
Sleeping volcano.
You are gold and rock as well.
You are gold: So conservative, moralistic

And dreamer of continuance of values.
My heart was clean while I begged your love.
Your heart was also clean to observe my love.
In your observation I became a trespasser.

But I had blue filled eyes to reflect the skies.
I had a mind filled with petals and fragrance.
But all these were meaningless
As you had your own eyes, skies and petals.

So you are pure gold, for sure.
But you are rock: So hard that no stream will
Flow to glow my parched land.
You paralyzed my feet, you had set fire to

My innocence and confidence.
You smashed my glassed heart and justified
Your action.
I admit in love's name that you are gold
And rock, you are virtue and vice....

I have been dwarfed by your moon's shine
How can I touch your chin so nice?

A LOVELY LOVELY

Snow came by
And you didn't budge
A sweet warm kiss
And you gave me frost

Warm was your heart
You gave my time
A diamond you are
You made me proud
Yourself denied

For me you gave
My plan you took
And precious you made
Alone i was never

Company you made
Your time you lost
For mine you caged
Hard you are

Laziness is afraid
On my toes, you keep
Never to fall, you hold
And still, my teacher you are

A lesson I'll never forget
Diamond is your heart
And a ring I'll hold you to me

MINE

Some hearts are diamond
But yours is more
You glitter your glow
Whenever you smile

A mother another
A friend more than
Love you give
Time cannot contest

Sweet food you cook
A taste to remember
Nine months you bear
A superwoman, it's clear

A cover you give
Beauty you make
Some hearts are diamond
But yours is better

Clearly Cut
God took his time
Not all can compete
That's why you're mine.

LOVE THAT LASTS

As I rummaged my books...
I found the poem you had written...
I feel blessed...it's still like I met you yesterday...

Nothing has still changed...
I preserve all that you have given...
How ineffectual I feel even today...
There is not a single way that I can repay...

Just remember...
How I missed you every single day.
It pleases me to write about you. .
Your success, your care, your smile, your touch...

Oh!! So much to say...
My dearest...
This day is most fitting and proper to celebrate and say
my love...
This is the tie that truly binds our hearts together...

Our lives are so interwoven that...
Whatever love of you...? I own today...
I dedicate it to you...

Copyright Madhuri Kulkarni

WHIRLPOOL OF EMOTIONS

OCEAN

Openness is the key for every relationship to succeed
No matter what circumstances,
Your feelings shall be heed
Conscientiousness reflect on the level of care shown
thru ups and downs

Valuing each other every moment of time, cheering up
like a clown
Extroverted one or an introvert in nature, no matter the
mood is,
Understanding is a good thing
Clashing of ideas with your dear

Agreeing to disagree is like a whirlpool where emotions'
sink
The hearts shall see and the
Minds shall intelligently think
Neurotic needs may go towards,

May go away or go against people
But what mostly deemed is that
All of us are uniquely lovable
Now my friend, let go of you emotions

Cry when you feel the need to cry
Laugh and live a life full of miracles
God is love and our hope of tower

EMOTIONS ARE ROLL UP

If my sense seeks
Some goodness justice
I will stay happiness
Stay just what I am

And be so coolest again
Whirlpool of emotions
Seeking some justice
To be whom I am

And I want to show
My goodness sense
World seeks me also
And I wish only now

To be chosen
My way and sense
Is goodness for me?
I need to be who I am

And I am trying only
To seek some justice
And be who I am
Forever.

Copyright Amb Maid Čorbić

TRANSFORM ME, PLEASE

Churning in a whirlpool of emotions
I struggle to swim in the endless eddy
Only to get back to the matrix of illusions
Where fog and mist play on clarity.

Kicking and flinging of limp limbs burdensome
The song of waters ceases to entice
Expected yoga calm never does come
Thousand nerves ache as if in splice.

Fear of being sucked down alive
Makes the feel of water terribly cold
My once strong heart forgets to strive
Meet needed hope has started to fold.

Rush of roiling flotsam down rocks
Builds up my fading consciousness
But something places me under myriad locks
Oh, I know it's a surge of sadness.

This may be my senseless end
I remember it was not long ago
When around was a thrill-joy blend
Where the heavens sparkle and glow.

Why should things change at a glance?
And do I have a choice when it's my glands
Malfunctioning to muddle my chance
To metamorphose in my chosen strands.

Should my choice be ever poor?
When I have listened to purified teachings
Yet remained a fool about to jump into a moor?
Lord, I am angry with me for my plethora of misgivings.

Copyright Loreta C Bande

GYRATION

A bundle of emotions gyrating us like a whirlpool in an ocean,
In a constant flux of mood swing,
Our emotions spontaneous reflux of inner streaming reflection,
Makes us victims of anger, sadness, joyfulness

And more we owe to our genetic or exotic influence,
Tears well up from eyes make us cry,
Seeing someone in distress,
Winning a match against a rival team,

Outburst of boundless joy we can't hold in.
Anger the fury emotional outburst,
Causes us much harm we can't measure.
Being emphatic or sympathetic to someone in need,

We mouth sweet juicy words to express our feelings for commiseration.
Emotions are all fine that defines us our being,
And groom our personality.
A balanced person with emotions well restrained,

Never does he break down in personal or impersonal loss,
Neither is he overjoyed by his gains.
He is like a calm sea waves rippling on the surface,
Emotions come like waves high and low tides,

But fail to gyrate him in the whirlpool of emotional flow.
Emotions act in a therapeutic way,
If one can cry in sadness,
Grief goes away with tears shed,

Heart becomes light.
Catheretic effects of tragic dramas best to define.

India.

EARTHLY STORMY WATERS

Human beings struggle
To understand
Life is a maelstrom
Destiny in command

We are swept along
From day to day
Tide often turns
Plans left in disarray

Kaleidoscope of emotions
Accompanies our journey
Mind stores experience
Creates a memory

Useful reserve
Guides individual existence
Forearmed follow
Path of least resistance

If sentiments surge
Threaten to overwhelm
We learn to place
Inner strength at the helm

Trust it to navigate
Earthly stormy waters
Drop, as necessary,
Stabilizing anchors

Do our best
In all conditions
To reach shore safely
If Fate commissions

WHIRLPOOL OF EMOTIONS

In the absence of mind
Absorbed deeply in thoughts
In the presence of love and sympathy
I have all the good will of humanity

No one in the world is perfect
God has all to reflect
We are to obey the one God
We are to pay for the sins before our lord

Love is the most precious thing
God has created all for the well-being
Hate is the worst thing that disturb peace
Create the environment full of harmony and peace

Fact and reality may be bitter
But it wins at end for the better
If there is justice there is peace
If there is rule of law there is justice

Say Welcome to the one who you meet
Bade farewell to all who you meet
Always say goodbye to the one who you left
Care for each other and never drift

Always do the right and keep everything in order
Be happy with your own happiness
Be kind to each other and never make people into
trouble
World is the place to live with dignity

World is a place to remain with discipline and tranquility
World is not the place to behave like stupid
Try again and again if you want to succeed

EMOTIONAL VORTEX

With a turbulent ocean inside,
Most often not naturally produced,
But created out of hatred, prejudices, frustrations,
Towards me, by my supposed loved ones,

Drowning yet not drowning,
In an overwhelming state of fighting emotions,
Why I survive every time, I wonder,
There's no point in coming out alive,

Only to meet those disgruntled figures,
Who had wished to see my corpse,
Had probably planned a grand celebration,
At the cost of my death, feigning tears,

Yet, I exist, for neither prayers get answered,
And, I find no route befitting me,
What shall I do? I wish to get submerged,
In the spinning waters of the emotional vortex,

Even if I yearn to come out fresh and clean,
With sparkling brightness and strength,
And, fulfill my dreams and goals,
I simply can't, in an environment,

Devoid of kind feelings towards me,
Where negativities rule supreme,
Where everyone's there, but none is mine,
A petrified and aghast me,

Longs for some solace, some hug,
That generous gentle touch,
But all I receive is an endless abyss,
A bitter turmoil I go through each day,
How long will it continue, let me see.

Copyright Amrita Mallik

MY LOVE IS DIFFERENT

My love is different, simple,
It is like a drop of rain
Filling with gentleness and warmth.
It is needed like air breathed.

There are no extreme comparisons,
Nor does it need a special name,
It takes over with lots of excitement and joy,
Goes with every hole like a wave.

Here, day and night wipe the borders,
There is no room for hatred or revenge,
A face overflowed with a smile,
You can simply feel it in the soul like a flood.

No convictions are needed,
Which know how to kill the spirit.
It finds the solution to each obstacle repeated,
And stands on the way to everyone,

Who tries to dig holes everywhere?
It is carried in the chest for long,
Because of it you have dreams for years,
It survives, perhaps

These colors of feelings make life's miracles.
Because of it, you stand firmly on the ground,
It is the treasure given,
Which unreservedly gives and

Lasts, continues and lasts...
The one who has it,
A better man becomes,
And never gives up...

Copyright Snežana Šolkotović

THOUGHTS AND EMOTIONS

Rejoicing
Amongst the gusty
All the while
Sitting, blissfully
In enchanting
Wind gaiety
A swirl of emotions and thoughts
Helixes in my mind
And I can barely swim on
When confusion reigns
And bewilderness holds
That one emotion
Which will keep me going on
Motivate me
Inspire me
And keep me right here
Make me strong
A fantasy of imaginativeness
Agreeable in sweet caress
Concealed in a drowse passion
In its very own creation
Deluding no attraction
Inside the cubicle of sight
Feeling sentiment
Reaction, affection
Response, sensation

TEMPESTUOUS VORTEX

There is an ocean
Deep inside my core
Containing, beside gems,
Beauties many more

Undulating waves
Drenching sandy shore
Needing love and peace
Seemingly implore

There are volcanoes
Active or dormant
Give rise to myriads
Restive sentiments

Happiness also
In my heart resides
There is force of love,
Deep inside, that, hides

These emotions swirl
And make me giddy
Move fast forming a
Turbulent eddy

The spiraling waves
Create objectives
With stormy angle
Bring new perspectives

This cosmos is run
By the omnipresent
And Supreme Power
That is omniscient

Copyright Sudha Dixit

WHAT CAN I SAY?

Tangled like the uncombed hair of a widow,
Confused like the mind of an insane...
Sometimes I wonder what's wrong with the
Race of Man...
The joy is never enough
Sadness is also tough
No matter what phase it is...
Every patch is so rough.
Why can't thee be content
And show gratitude for come what may.....
What can I say?
I am judging non but myself
For these thoughts swirl within me
I keep looking for answers
That never seem to be.
I hope by venting I shall find release
Be content and be at ease ....with whatever potion.....
I shall survive this whirlpool of Emotions...Amen

Copyright Akila Shariff
Kenya

JOY

I would love to joy if your cloth still suits me
I have been taken for granted on my to seek you
You played hide-and-seek so well
I got tired and went to my abode of struggles

If you would find me, do not go far, I am in sadness
I currently dwell freely in his mansion

SADNESS
Sadness, if I must spend the day in your abode
Do not make me tarry till night
So the sorrowful heart might have a good mare
My eyes are already a desert, I have sold my tears for fear of another day

FEAR,
Fear, I once saw you fall Goliath instead of small David
Then I knew how cunning little you are
Why spare that powerless little and prey the powerful mighty?
My regards to death, you must tell her how motherly she is
Tell how much sadness embraced me in love
Also not forget how joy refused to come out of his hiding place

DEATH,
If you must lay your icy hand on the king
Do not but do the poor tender
We do not strive with wealth, let we peaceful rest
Maybe you leave us to go on our will
A dead man shouldn't die again
While death tarries,
I am anxious about mother Earth
Hope there is a resting place made ready?
My back aches for trekking to and fro heaven to earth
Prepare me my duvet, a sumptuous dinner and at least a wooden bed
While I am anxious, I must pack my loads I might soon take turn

DON'T TAKE IN HEART

It's all about feelings
Of dear mind.
Tidal mirth
For dealing
The precious part of life.

Sometimes good
Sometimes bad
Sometimes jolly
Sometimes stop
On a mournful state.

It's fine
Swirling thoughts
Myriad hues
Eternal clue
For desired crew
Dancing emotions
For controlling
Life's motion.

Then hold this moment
Make your comment
No more worries
Glory... flowing...wave of life
As a glowing star
In dark night.

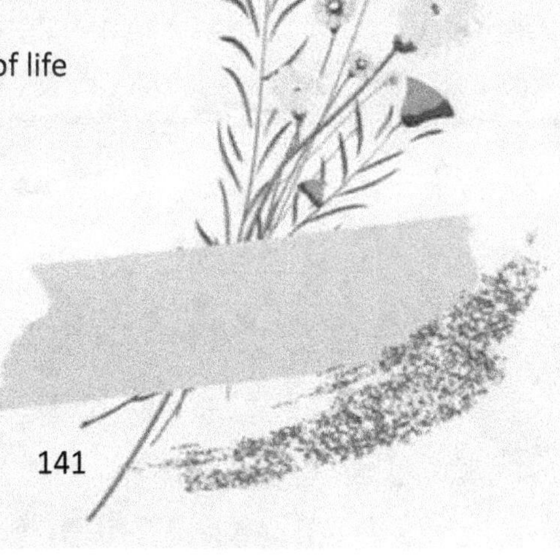

WHIRLPOOL OF EMOTIONS

Once, I watered barren fields
Waited for the flowers to blossom
The farmer looked from afar
Cherishing blessed hands
Yet the farmer could not stay
Sadly, he passed away
The wolf jumped and snatched the buds
They denied me their scent
And run away from my tent, what shall I say?
Cast away in a whirlpool of emotions
Shall I with anger, their hatred repay?
Or could I sneak and look for
Some pity in their hearts and knock on their door?
Sometimes, I rush and get a wash with tears
Sometimes despondency shares my fears
Sometimes I beg the sky to erase the clouds
A gleam of joy my heart finds
Yet; some thorns still prick
How could a generous hand be beaten by a stick?

AMBA-GLORIA

A woman Pregnant
Yet force to labour
To eat, to drink
And still feed another
Her feet grew tired
As everyday was on repeat
The farm too far
A distance walked was a drain
On her way back
Were eyes moving by
None to help
As they stole while she was asleep
Her work gone
Another pain to serve
A kick came by
The midwife
Passing by
Alerted by her screams
Ran
Dropping all what they held
Even the glass had to be broken
Holding her, holding out the screams
The pain finally dropped
Pushing out all that had made her suffer
A child born to world that ignored
With open cries, it took its first breath

Taken away, the blood washed away
Given a clean body, it was free atlas
And to her mother's face
She was laid
Ambo was her name
Precious, it was indeed Amber
And her glory was yet to be seen
Her mother smiled as all watched.

DANCE OF THE LUSTY LOVER

Push... Pull
Jump... Through
Scratch... Kick
Drag... Throw
And that was it.
Tears flowed
As the moment walked away
Looking back
As the eyes blinked away
That was it.
All my voice bottled up
In my head
Another note to the book of pain
My movements held
I couldn't stand again
All the love lost
It all turned to pain
Sleep was stolen from me
A line crossed in veins
Choking my blood
It all clotted in reign
Fear was the game
I was lost in its play
Shadows move out of ray
Patterns were no longer the same
Was it a dream or a play?
Anxiety was my read
Paranoia was my change

Voiceless
I spoke not
Who would believe
When all was makeup
And plastic?
When all was a smile
That paid the bill?
A choice i made
The wrong love i lusted for
A mistake i defended
The price i pay
Speaking would be my shame.

WHY DID IT HAPPEN

Turmoil of thoughts, nightmare of emotions
I roll side, suffering and masks of pain
Tears shed, flooding my pillow as rain
Why, once in a while this happens to me

It has been a long time we are apart
You left me behind without knowing bye
Shall I think you suffering in pain, too?
We had so many crazy nights of love

Whispers, in ears my melodious words
I listening to, you repetition
Once, twice and many at a times, am I wrong
Betrayal of mind, I don't know reason

I thought it was forever love of us
In a wink of eyes, it was all over
You went away, mourning my fate, unjust
It was true love baby it could come closer

If you had let me know about your plan
Prepared heart of mine for the dismissal
No presence of you, dear, in a short time
Perhaps, I wouldn't shed tears of betrayal

It was betrayal leaving without words
Don't tell me you be a coward or fiend
While beside me you standing, sea of roses
Was; then, salty waters which make you wilt

Lots of vegetation grow in the sea
Colorful fishes crossing side to sides
Seasoning the environment with glee
It was your love for me, baby, that was fake

O' insensible heart, a stone on chest
You agglomerate with grains of pearled sand
While heart of mine bleeds from your aloofness
From what I had, now I don't understand

Copyright Maria Elvira Fernandes Correia

LOVE ME WITHOUT CONDITIONS

You say you want to go away,
I don't want to hear you say goodbye,
Many nights I have stayed awake,
Thinking of my own mistake,

You want to have me replaced,
And leave me feeling misplaced,
There are things we cannot expose,
Because they'll appear like a curse,

I cannot stand the embarrassment,
Of you treating me like an ornament,
I also have emotions,
You should love me without conditions,

I know that I have treated you wrong,
But there's a way to move along,
I don't want you to leave me alone,
I cannot stand the pain when you're gone,

The music would seem meaningless,
No one would understand my sadness,
There's a way to have this settled,
I know you feel belittled,

But I have given you all my respect,
If you don't understand what do you expect,
I am ready to forgive,
With my actions I'll prove,

Without you it's like living with no air,
You we are such a wonderful pair,
My heart is breaking into pieces,
My body is hurting many places,

The thought of us apart sounds like death,
It's not time for me to leave earth,
Baby I had given you all of my trust,
Please stay and make our love to last.

SORROWS OF LOVE

I want to be with you every day
And we write the first episode of our story
Watching those love scenes we always share
Embracing the wind as it blows with care

Everyone wants to keep the best moments
In every sweet stare and comments
Save them in the secret part of the memory
Till the never-ending finale of our own love story.

Staying together as the years roll on
Even the season of winter and spring is born
Don't want to make choices and we can't give up it seems
For the nights we were both in dreams.

No one wants to listen to the lonely song of the moon
Even the snowflakes swirl in slow motion
We keep some memories while our time flies
Even the stars shut their eyes in the sky.

Like the whirlpool of emotions
I can't control my own
The sound of silence keeps on calling
The feelings keep longing and bearing.

The sorrows of love
Like the ocean, unpredictable and wide
Beyond the blue lagoon and beneath the horizon
Love is eternal, the reason we keep moving on.

DID SHE COMES BACK!?

A simple glimpse, while I'm in pain,
Yet you stay, and resides in my brain.
My tears seem to dwindle and wane,
To my grief, are you the angel to contain?

Coz in your glance, as I turn around,
A familiar smile, is what I found.
In a flash a memory came unannounced,
Who are you, for shaking my ground?

For when she's gone, I've made a promise,
Never my heart, will sought a new bliss.
But fate it seems is concocting a twist,
My solemn vow is on the verge of demise.

For your allure already conquers my pride,
Not my mind, but my heart now decides.
I've broken my words, dried the tears I cried,
A weird peculiar love seems to come alive.

You stir my emotion that is trying to forget
The sorrow that I thought I can never reset.
You're a whirlpool, sucking me to your depth,
That I can't avoid, and is ruining my pledge.

You're a whirlwind, carrying me as you swirl,
I'm drifting and being drawn to your sphere.
A surprise occurrence that is giving me chill,
Declined by you, is now my greatest fear.

For it looks like my angel has made you good,
Coz you're like her, whom I so adored.
In you, I found the warmth I am inured,
I now feel that my oath, to you, has detoured.

What I wanted now is it's you I should love
In my mind, the sacrifice is worth your heart
The thing I missed, appears to be shaping up
The love I wished, is you, coming back to life.

Copyright Nathaniel D. Cruz

LET'S THINK REASONABLE

My emotion bursts uncontrollable
Like the wild sea swallows everything
Swaying bad temper unreasonable
I just wish to release pain by crying

I move as the biggest flood
Moving to destroy the wall of city
Mind has high tension as boiling blood
Blaming all as the cause of complexticity

You are the one I really love
Breaking my heart so pain
I know nothing how to move
All look dark and just the rhythm of rain

Have you never imagined?
If it happens in your life
Can you smile without feeling hatred?
Enjoying the excitement for being safe

I'm sure you will be despair
Facing the betrayal before your eyes
May be you think that I am not fair
Let you pour blue tears

If you give me chance once again
I want to build the castle of happiness
Living and loving to forget deep pain
Filling the life with true gladness

Please keep calm to control our emotion
God gives love to all of his creation.

Copy right Gatot Malaisianto
Indonesia

THE WHIRLPOOL OF LOVE

Anxiety has played out
To the abyss of wishes
Thoughts that are going viral
You are ambits there

Kill them on the illusion
With a carved face
For the love of the created
Lonely God
On the cliff sighs

Tailoring a glorious dream
Go drown the bird
Happy birthday ivici
From the iceberg

Love is melting him down
On a whirlpool of passion
Promises the winter of the soul
Drops are falling down

Into the closed water
The sun is smiling
Mesmerized by the beauty
Emotions are floating around

In a timeless story
Hugs to the helm's
They are drowning in their eyes
Azure colors

The discontent is extinguished
By the power of dreams
Awakened by the dawn
The waves have been quiet

Calm sea
Up with the clueless
Of a long time wandering
To the endless hope.

Copyright Duška Kontić
Montenegro

EMOTIONAL BATTLE

She was crying and shouting
On the shores of stormy sea
Where only she could hear herself
Voice remained buried in her throat

Watching the rage of giant waves
Echoing miserably within herself
Making her motionless
Unfathomable fathoms

Sighs of grief
One on top of the other
Like layers of shells and sand
In a piece of limestone

Both becoming the same element
She couldn't winnow out
One from the other
Knowing not how to proceed further

Regretted for not raging against
The atrocities and deceptions
Pushing her into such violent waters
Furious rage after drowning made not much difference

Haphazard movement of emotions
Turbulent memories
Made her feel dizzy
In sleep and wakefulness

She was caught in the storm
Howling round about
And she hardly knew who she was!

WHEN YOU'RE IN LOVE

The love in your heart paints dreams.
His/her eyes are reflected in the mirror.
On the wings of love your soul flies.
Butterfly wings flutter in your stomach.
A smile on your lips blooms.
A whirlpool of emotions is in your heart.

WHIRLPOOL OF EMOTIONS

Emotions swirls
Hillside is coloured in autumn hues
Swirling waves of emotions
Empty and detached

I stand as an autumn tree
Breeze is cold against skin
Tickle my senses deep
I ask wind 'bout your path

I gasp that air, unable to breathe.
Ridiculous, I try to swallow my pains
Sob inconsolably as a child
Whilst emotions swirls

Burst out in multitude
As a tornado
Not in rhythmic beats
This turmoil is drowning me deep

In matrix of disappointment
I try to take a plunge
Breathe and survive
To love, or to be loved

I have no clue?
I'm numb and frozen.
Paranoid or twisted?
Finally I realize

Emotions can't drown me.
I'll float as a lotus
With my roots grounded in waterbed
O' my heart be holistic
Cool, calm, and untangled free of sufferings.

Copyright Anjana Prasad

EMOTIONS ARE BASIS OF LIFE

Emotions are life
They are also strife
Without these Emotions
Life is like sharp knife
Emotions are relations
Emotions are passions
Emotions are true mission
Emotionless men are tension
Emotions are teacher
Emotions are preacher
Emotions are highest God
Emotions are sentiment bond
Emotions are great
Emotions are threat
Emotions are ever sweet
Emotions are inner tweet
Emotions in you
Emotions in me
Emotions in them
Emotions are same
Emotions true
Emotions false
Emotions are Emotions
If someone else
Emotions are our heritage
They are life history it's page
Emotions are life-test
Keep emotions but rest

ENTER THE STORM

Woman, I can tell you are lonely and bored to death
I see the weariness written all over your face
I can read it in the dreamy look of your eyes
You want a man who can thrill you

In a whole new way
Woman, what you are looking for
Can be found in me
I can take you where

Your fantasies are fulfilled
In the island of pleasure
Where desires are satisfied
Why cocoon your feelings in thunderous silence?

I want to stir up the tempest in your heart
And enter the storm with you
Body, soul and mind
When the love tornado sweeps us off

To the heights of passion
We'll be spinning in ecstasy
Like Michael Jackson on the dancefloor
Floating above this ephemeral world.

THE HEART IS NEVER STILL

It's the seat of emotions,
Constantly turbulent, always buoyant,
It's a whirlpool of passions.

Quiet, my beating heart,
Why are you so restless?
Why do you tirelessly
Flow in and flow out

Like a heaving sea?
Why do waves of emotions
Always engulf me?
The emotional ebb and tide will never cease,

This warm heart will never freeze,
Till my last breath,
And what after death?
Where do these emotions fly?

Where will they go and
Laugh and cry?
Oh this whirlpool is like a warm blanket,
That covers my life, from moment to moment,

I would rather be warm and emotional
Than frigid and cold hearted;
I would rather be joyful or sorrowful,
Than indifferent and hard hearted;
Let me be soft and loving,
Than someone who is afraid of giving.

SUCKED INTO A MAELSTROM OF EMOTIONS

Experiencing a conundrum is the inner soul
Serpentine is my journey
Obscure is the path
Lava is bubbling inside me,

And yearns to explode
But, it is silence that I choose
As I fear the outcome
Depression engulfs me like the tentacles of an octopus

And the misery seems insurmountable
Yet, I try hard every day
To wriggle out of the pit
I have to conquer my fears

And will surely reach the pinnacle
Clarity I will slowly have
If I am ready to combat the haziness
Evanesced peace will surely return

My face would once again shimmer
Metamorphosis will happen
If I develop the courage to silence the turbulence
I would no longer be the raging ocean

But a harbinger of hope and happiness
Seeing this new ME
On everyone's face,
Will appear a glee

EMOTIONS EDDYING

Doing with the known is emotion;
Not one's truth but the truth is vision, inborn.
O Reality in its totality suffers from relativity;
To have true trueness one's search ends in eternity.

Emotion a mirage drawn between truth and falsity;
Emotion one's life's moving energy to have an entity.
Mind as emotion's tool reveals in conditions, triangle;
'What makes a human?' is lost to a state, fully riddled.

In trait and texture as emotions do inborn differ;
As noble, ignoble and indifferent they form nature.
Divinity's veiled path hangs one between real and unreal
The matter or the spirit's realm's gravity makes one whirl?

Intellect as judge does pendulant between subtle and gross;
Heart's thoughts' design, triangular innately shadow desires.
Divinity within as fire or mirror, prefer to be smoke or dust Clad;
Of gradual folding states from being pure to semi-pure to impure.

Emitted whatever is destined to return back to the root
Emotions harmonious or not yield to have God's image's trait.
O one's nature, true thirsts to be circled back into itself
But brain overheats, heart troubles and body deranges
Relativity, contradiction, inversion, conditions, opposing

O mind, a safe Harbor of the devil guided negative feeling
Complex, superiority or not moves one to improvement of self;
Angelic strive within leads one to conform peace and Stillness.
Despite one's reality cross purposed and one's experience mix bagged
Angels' twelve legions plus divine love's prowess are timely aided.

FISTFUL HEART'S MANOEUVRES

I heave and blob, rise and fall
Sink and swim in overwhelmed stupor
I brush past agony and rapture
Stumped helpless at my nemesis blooper.

I'm sucked in a roaring melting pot
That whirs and churns my existence
In a vortex constant as days turn nights
And seasons parade in precision intense.

Hamlets turn to ghosts in retribution
Battle cries perforate the sky riled
Jealousy unfangs evil, death-beds shiver
A furious response to every emotion wild.

What is life but a weaver's tale?
Of magic and mystery spun effortless
That come in spasms in every story
Whizzing past from birth to death endless.

The drama continual throws and spins
Bouts of heartaches, dismays ample
Yet the stage set stays unchallenged
Players march in and march out to trample

Emotions that rock and squeeze
Fistful hearts lavish maneuvers
I float on uncontrolled, hapless
In the whirlpool of emotion- brewer.

FOUNTAINS OF EMOTION

It's strong, it's fast,
I can't lay a hold of it.
I can't stop it, I can't control it,
Neither do I understand its mechanism,

It's way bigger than me.
It swept away my feet
And threw me into the deep.
It drowned me in it

But I refused to swim
And my willpower I summoned not
To surface and catch a breath
For I suffocated not.

Slowly I went down
Sinking everyday
But to nothing else
In this world do I care?

For sweet lies the death ahead
That I shot my eyes to the world and waited
For the pleasures of forever with a smile.
But the pool is whirling again

And I never saw it coming
Now it's suffocating
Promising not a happy ending
And out of the cool spout

Of healing and soothing balm
Now comes a hot and scotching lava.
Help me, save me, someone
How did I miss the points?

How did I got it wrong,
Save me now, before I die.
#I'M C.I.

Copyright Chiedozie .I. Chinagorom

CAUGHT IN THE WEB

Lavish me with attention
I still feel the shimmer and the quiver
In the deepest recesses of my core
As air stirs ruthlessly

Putting an end to merciful breeze
Help me overcome the arid acres of distress
And burst into a soulful song
Before horizon blurs in the edge

Prepares to fold itself
And hide under the pleats of darkness
Eventually gets wrapped under night's flair
Take a long pause ...if you so want

But whisper something in a hush
The waves of gnawing sense
Now crashing and washing my bare feet
Would snatch my breath

And lull me soon.... it seems
There has been enough comeuppance
For my misgiving
Spare me from the wrath this time

I am waiting with a pale ache
Wishing for the darkness to evanescence
Enabling me to embrace the perpetual sun
Hope your gesture proffers a long day

Wide and clear
Assures a gleaming night
With moths and fireflies dancing
To the rhythms of elation

At a remote corner of earth's fringe
I stand ...clinging to a flicker of hope
Looking at the bees bustle and hum
The butterflies heave and clamber
Cherishing a desire to live a life as before.

Copyright Sonata Dash

LOVE IS PIVOTAL EMOTION

Man a bundle of feelings, emotions, desires
Sea of emotions, is man, full of desire which are always on fire
Right from childhood, saw people run after pleasure
Desire makes us overcome, hurdles realities, to seek leisure.
Emotions, when awakened, churn minds, give birth
To temptations, jealousy, arrogance greed, sadness, deceit, mirth
Human life becomes, sea of desires to achieve
Rat race, to achieve, use unfair foul means to win, conceive.
Wear masks of love, bliss, tolerance, we cheat
Winning running after mirages, whole life chase, cheat, greet
Born to fulfill roles, reach goals, to achieve
Make life meaningful, live happily, we all agree.
Desire to win, gets us entangled in web of emotions
To achieve ends, use fowl, unfair means, and actions
Use others, as stepping stones, with arrogance, conceit
Robbing the meek, innocent, use them as means of deceit.
Demons of mind, tempt minds with desires, to fulfill needs
Even what they don't need, jealous souls, grabs from hard workers, due to greed
Pain they inflict, gives them sadistic pleasure, to their souls
Put others down, to lose a will to live, as they've lost their aims, goals.
When the false masks fall, harsh realities are bared

Naked, false, because masks, are masks, must fall apart, burn
Burn in the realities, truth's, hearth of life
Life that's clean, pristine, love to live and let live, without strife.
A love that is bliss, Divine, a blessing to enjoy
Great saints, once full of desires, to live life in joy
Overcame them with tolerance, friendship, contemplation, love
People labelled them as failures, they achieved, peace of mind as doves.
Doves to spread messages of peace, love, friendship, share, care, over earth
Labelled as saints, once overcame bad deeds, emotions, now preach, so all live in mirth
Thought how much does a man need to live in joy and peace?
Why countries fight for God's bounties, sink in emotional pools of divide, to live in pieces.

WHIRLPOOL OF EMOTIONS

You came I was wrapped in captivating emotions.
I shivered when you call my name,
My passion and desire at its highest peak;
I quivered in your passionate embrace...

As we savour this moment's bliss...
I couldn't live again without your love
In the labyrinth of all my fantasies and dreams
Within this blazing reality of contentment.

We go berserk in the sweetness of love
So we cuddle.our powerful dreams
To give our lives more beauty and grace
To bask in the freedom of this universe.

To glorify our existence within God's blessings
To cherish this precious life, we need strength
To save us from weaker dreams
Thus no value to comprehend...

Within this whirlpool of emotions my heart does not lie;
I'll rekindle all the dying embers of hope and courage...
To replenish our ethereal energies.
To be able to heal and generate happiness

For all mankind, for all the seasons...
To fill every void of longings,
To sing songs of life devoid of pain
To live in peace, with compassion and kindness

To be grateful that there's one universe of love
In the wilderness of our every dream
Making our lives complete.

God is love, God is Peace
Our prayers are blest; we can only know
Salvation in God's embrace.

Copyright Med Villapando

UNCONTROLLABLE HEART

In the middle of the night, I contemplate
When my life toss by conflicting currents
Panting, my heart is over my troubled mind
Ruled by the immense impact of emotion

Despising what is truth and what is right
Blinded by my fervor and excitement
Lost in colliding forces of real and unreal
Living in clouds under the rocky road

Surviving the odds and worries
I was dazed and confused by my heart.
Love captured my once sullen mood,
Trapped in the unbounded sentiments

Hypnotizing my whole senses to the oblivion
My mind is floating, as my body responded
Ignoring the people around me.
My insouciant response drive me away

To the people who love me the most
Carried by this egotistical emotion
Putting myself into devastating dignity
The bondage that must lose to set me free

Complicated love tends to drown our life
A vortex swallowing that is hard to survive
Down to the deep in the unconscious mind
Lost in the parallel of what true love is.

A conscientious heart ruled by a rightful mind
Never take a poison to ruin his life.
Love is perfect as long it is right
Play with emotion but never with fire.

Copyright Dolo Rez

PONDER OVER

Annoyance hugged me tightly
Alluring me with its magic nicely
As I didn't tell it that I am mortal
Frustration's friendly move fondled me

Far from wisdom land we went for a long drive
I could hardly come back, fault was mine, and I didn't tell it that I am a mere mortal
Fear was my dearest neighbor

We had always kept off from our family member, fearlessness!
Our strong bond didn't ever let me meet anyone around, I felt, I had to live and without my dearest neighbour, I might not live at all!

I took tuition from ignorance
It taught me everything to remain a fool forever
I could not accept anyone but fools, thereafter! I could never appreciate except for fools!
By the time I knew that I could have had better choice, I was in mess!

I drank tears, I tasted insults but I couldn't break the shell I lived in!
When I breathed my last, all knew that I was engulfed by the whirlpool of emotions
Evil emotions endless endearment ended my life before I could live it!
Physical fitness too can't save you, if we are engulfed by emotional imbalances!

Pain- pleasure , success - failure and love- hate ought to be balanced before they take grip of us!
Tell each of your emotions that you are living life with a guarantee card of death!
Tell your emotions that you hardly have time to live with them!
Let them not engulf you
Let them not please you

Copyright Rajani Mula

HAIKU

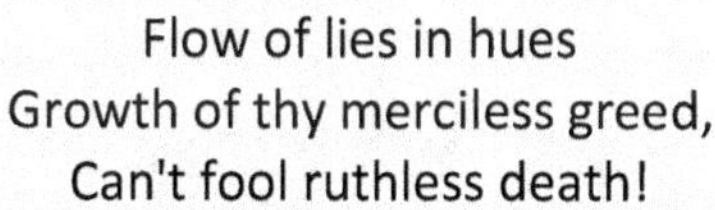

Flow of lies in hues
Growth of thy merciless greed,
Can't fool ruthless death!

Copyright Rajani Mula

purple reflections
sky and stream mirroring peace
nature in a trance

Copyright Loreta C Bande

River flows calmly
Reflecting hues around it
Ain't it magical

Copyright Karta V

Hear me, dear heavens
calm my rivers and my plains
let only peace reigns.

Copyright Nathaniel D. Cruz

Of prestine water
Shaded with the deep blue skies
The beauty of nature

Copyright Vicente A.Valdez.Jr.

A nice scene to see
Calm and serene prevail here
River, land and sky call.

Copyright Prashanta Kumar Samanta

Splendid be thy light,
Mirrored in soft cotton streams,
Winding through the trees.

Copyright Vee Barnes

beneath purple clouds
life is in serenity
charming beauty.

Copyright Rhoda Tomelden

Trees, clouds and flowers,
Reflecting their inner soul,
In the calm river.

Copyright Nooriyah Karimi

by a vibrant brook
myriad flowers in bloom
is a soothing view

Copyright Mayyu Hamim

beauty's influence
palette of peace for the soul
Autographed by God

Copyright Pamela Tennant

A purple passion
Lyrics in blue petals
Pining skies

Copyright Nandita De

Still silent waters
With the sun bidding adieu
Aeolian sound echoes.

Copyright Rhodora Garcia-Medina

Lilac hues shine bright
Blushing
Nature's reflections

Copyright Davi Ramphal Rampersad

Nature's tranquil hues
Soft lavender tones aglow
Embrace the spirit

Copyright Margaret Karim

A very beautiful sunset sky,
As the peaceful sweet waters flow by,
I desire this feeling everyday.

Copyright Kenneth Munene

moments of silence
The still waters to soothe
One's heart, mind and soul

Copyright Ratanang Seepapitso

Purple clouds whisper
lavender words on river.
listen with my soul.

Copyright Edmon Libres

A dense, green jungle
A flowing stream mirroring
Purple hues of cloud

Copyright Sudha Dixit

Nature breathes us life
God made all things beautiful
Love and care grip them

Copyright Teresita Barrera

Dispirited soul
Immaculately bring soothe
Through nature's magic

Copyright Marivic C. Miranda

The magenta splash
Upon horizon's flat walls,
Touch of nature's best!

Copyright Obingo Wesonga

Qetesi nate,
rrjedh si ky lum i fushes,
krejte ngadale.

Copyright Ollga Farmacistja

Lavender is love
purple nurtures nature
serene lilac skies

Copyright Lubna Ahmed

Brook cut green meadows
Above in sky sort of hues
Lamina glass flow

Copyright Maria Elvira Fernandes Correia

purplish sky Greenfields
reflects on the still river
merging hues of blues

Copyright Lucy A. Mendiola

Sky lends a bevy of hues
canvas of earth soaks each ounce
cosy ambience hunches over

Copyright Sujata Dash

Glorious Creation,
All made from God's skillful hands,
It brings solitude!

Copyright Gina Gela Maristela

Nature's calling me
Its exquisite loveliness
In my heart and soul.

Copyright Medy Villapando

Nature's beauty
Harmony of greens, and blue
It's God's hands at work.

Copyright Chandra Sekhar Batabyal

A Lavender Haze...
And Upon the water gaze...
Nice beyond in many ways...

Copyright The Ono

Stunning nature heals,
Satiates the empty soul.
A proof of God's love.

Copyright Maria Editha Garma-Respicio

Python crawls on grass
Woods and sky are spectators
Snake charmer's magic.

Copyright Kishor Kumar Mishra

Luring lush fresh greens.
Calming purple, streams and blues.
Hail my peace and bliss

Copyright Marvin Marcelino

Mauve color of sky
Depicted tint by water
Somber mood meadow

Copyright Ency Bearis

Green, blue, red, purple,
So many colours scattered,
Convas of Nature.

Copyright Gopal Sinha,

River flows calmly
Where the abundance of grace
Lies in paradise.

Copyright Gloria A. Yu

Warm splendid morn sees
O' beams of eclipsing hues
Phantom daylight gems

Copyright Daniel Miltz

Nature opens heart
Reflection of dreamy mart
Mysterious art.

Copyright S Afrose

Gentle mauve rippling
Above and below, scattered
Blues sway, on the Green

Copyright Shamain Simeon

Nature changes hue
As per season's righteous due
Aura revolves in queue.

Copyright Dr.Sailabala Dash

It denotes riddles
Cultivating a deep link
Nature's odyssey.

Copyright Rosie B. Licudo

Stream slows down its pace
One lovely winter morning
Nature in rapture

Copyright B.S.Saroja

Sing, tiny flowers,
hymns to endless skies above,
beauty is your voice.

Copyright Joscephine Gomez

Romance in the air
The earth wearing sky's colour
Wondrous is nature

Copyright Vijaya Sarmah

the hues of the day
my bed lilac and heather
reflecting colors

Copyright Rose Huy Woolket.

Mauve hue reflection
Melting into the green
Nature's abundance grace

Copyright Pagan Parimita Nanda

serene clime allures
bewitches us, take us beyond
the maddening crowd

Copyright Seema Sharma

landscape of Nature
that touches my very core
enhancing myself

Copyright Jaya Karmalkar

the pellucid lake
holding her breath like a seer
for lavender sky.

Copyright Mousumee Baruah

Purple wondrous sky
Gives me solace when I'm sad
Soothes my heart and mind

Copyright Gloria Magallanes-Loeb

You melted too soon,
Be with me, my only need;
For you my heart bleeds.

Copyright Jyotirmoy Ghosal

colourful flowers
smile, sing, shine, on banks of stream
lovely God's haven.

Copyright Vinod Singh

Loving green jungle
Morning dew shows wondrous place
The river flows love

Copyright Gatot Malaisianto

And the winter comes
old fragrance is here to stay
love is ethernal

Copyright Amb Maid Čorbić

Mystic purple sky
Sings with fragrant bluebeard bud
Into the nigh gloom

Copyright Jem Maleon

painted purple clouds
nature watching reflection
perfect creation

Copyright Dolo Rez

River water bright
Blossoms adorn in clusters
Calm, therapeutic

Copyright Anjana Prasad

reflecting the sky
bright on the earth's surface
swimming as in tranquil stream

Copyright Mohammed Toyob Khan

Sky lights up in pink
Casts over fields and water
Good days up ahead

Copyright Azucena Libiran Gonzales

Natures poetic art
A sense of sorrow and hope
Peculiar Beauty

under cosmic skies
deep waters are stirred up
new waves of thought

tweetku

Busy reaching for stars
Chasing the moon
Forgetting to live while alive.

Copyright Vee Barnes

Totem built to reach the moon...
As we reach out...
Before light gone soon

Copyright Tha Ono

Nate e bukur
ma ruaj kujtimin e mikut te humbur
ma ruaj aromen e shpirtit te tij der sa te vij.

Copyright Ollga Farmacistja

Stars aren't far
What matters is your dare
And determination to cross all bars

Copyright Ritu Kamra Kumar

Dreams:
They do shine
Even in darkest night

Copyright Alvin Agena Andino

Moon like a tiny bulb,
facinating me to catch hold of it
and having it within my reach.

Copyright Anu Gupta

Too far yet too near
Little by little
Soon I will be there.

Copyright Gloria A. Yu

Moon is in your hand
If with will your goal is high
But your feet are on land

Copyright Dr Karu Kala-Mohan Jamda

My little hands try,
To reach the sky...
Though the moon/goal is high...

Copyright Madhuri Kulkarni

If I could reach the Moon...
I'd shrink it to bulb size,
Moonlight, room my.

Copyright Maria Elvira Fernandes Correia

Find a balance,
No matter the circumstances,
And you'll reach your dreams.

Copyright Kenneth Munene

No matter how unreachable
Your dreams are-
Faith matters

Copyright Ming Gaspi Gaton

As life to reach the dreamed moon,
Stretch a reach too
For spiritual sanctity.

Copyright Loreta C Bande

No hurdles or dangers
Could ever stop me,
til' I tightly grasp my destiny.

Copyright Marvin Marcelino

A child's mind treats
All fantasies as real
While adults' turn emotions to reel

Copyright Dr. Rodrigo M Dantay Jr

Age is not a bar
Education is light
Helps you reach great heights.

Copyright Anjana Prasad

Imagine a sky
Alight with hope
Ensure dreams never die

Copyright Margaret Karim

Like looming moon
Illuminating fertile mind
Rests wandering heart...

Copyright Manmohan Rajbanshi

Step by step, through much trouble
Even a child can snatch
The yonder sun.

Copyright Mafizuddin Chowdhury

The moon comes
Within reach to play
With the innocent child.

Copyright Gopal Sinha,

With courage and persistence
I will build a ladder
To your dreams.

Copyright Silviya Veselinova

Success, a boon
It's like in the moon
That needs grit, patience to reach

Copyright Ency Bearis

With a carefree touch
On my mind, my eyes
Are tagged on the price!

Copyright Obingo Wesonga

A bulb looks like moon
My hands try to reach it out
By all means using chairs

Copyright Zenaida Laragan Taloza

We are little children
Innocent in understanding
And too tiny to know everything!

Copyright Tess Ritumalta

Wish I were child again
To aim without negativity
To have nothing but amity!

Copyright Rajani Mula

Step a step I am to rise
To reach the target
Seems so high.

Copyright Chandra Sekhar Batabyal

Ladder for Moon
Sky is limit
To stay pretty

Copyright Amb Maid Čorbić

Reaching high night sky
Above a floating moon lie
Heaven smiles at ye'

Copyright Daniel Miltz

Touch the zenith
Enduring all barriers
Yonder isn't the sky;
Neither thy enthusiasm less.

Copyright Seema Sharma

#Tweeku38
You can get the light,
With child's innocence,
And will to go through hurdles...

Copyright Deepa Vankudre

A child can touch the moon
If we give faith
And trust on him soon

Copyright Kanduri Charan Rout

Focus on the goal
Come what may
Through hell or highwater

Copyright Davi Ramphal Rampersad

Dreams exist like the moon
Glowing, teetering at my fingertips
But full of challenges.

Copyright Janet Licudo

Step by step I'll climb
Build my home in the sky
Fanciful dreams fly me to the moon

Copyright Lucy A. Mendiola

Naive birds dream of,
Under their woolly mother
The sky isn't the limit.

Copyright Mayyu Hamim

I thought the moon was mine
To give to you,
Not my best idea.

Copyright Josh Hodgepodge

Moon shines above,
Like a bulb within my hand
Enthralled my heart with love.

Copyright Ben-hur Sistoso

Aiming high
To get light in life
Would face a series of difficulties.

Copyright Mohammed Rashid Ali.

If I could reach the moon's serenity
It would be a touch of peaceful rendezvous
To seek my lunatic asylum.

Copyright Vicente A. Valdez. Jr

Aspire high
Have faith and patience
Nothing is impossible.

Copyright Kishor Kumar Mishra

No ladder, no ropeway
Yet, obsessed with Moon
I'll have some solution soon.

Copyright Sudha Dixit

Reaching it so near
To tiptoe leaps and bounds
Just don't fall

Copyright Gloria Magallanes-Loeb

Dreams are in the moon
Only need to balance your feet
To reach it.

Copyright Vijaya Sarmah

An infant child,
Being attracted by glowing globe,
Makes extra efforts towards its brightness

Copyright Okoi Amadiowei Jacob

Love will be the ladder
That will lead me
To the moon itself.

Copyright Snežana Šolkotović

Driven by will and light
Ready to step sky battlefields
And win the hardest fight

Copyright Sihem Cherif

The moon is not so high
It can be touched
The girl thinks so.

Copyright Prashanta Kumar Samanta

Dream big
Start little by little
Later you will be there

Copyright Harold Vite

Tweetku48
Reaching for impossible dreams
Can be very challenging
But we'll listen to our hearts.

Copyright Medy Villapando

The ladder of blessing knowledge
Gives wings of hope
To reach the moon

Copyright Gatot Malaisianto

With innocence, pure
With deep love and longing
The Alone aspires for the Alone.

Copyright Dr Amiya Rout

Kids will do everything
They think is possible
To reach for the moon and back.

Copyright Rhodora Garcia-Medina

A young little mind,
Eager to find,
The truth amongst all lies.

Copyright Nooriyah Karimi

Small steps taken, balance
In dreams of Luna shine
There for the taking

Copyright Shamain Simeon

Hopefully, aspire to reach, moon
Unbalanced chairs, difficult position
Learn life's lesson, then achieve.

Copyright Vinod Singh

Careful how you dream
Be anxious what you dreamed of
Then reach for it

Copyright Nathaniel D. Cruz

A messy beginnings
But keep your faith within
And keep on going.

Copyright Rhoda Rumbaua

Dreamers never lose their naivety
Making them a novelty
In the world of reality.

Copyright Liege Lord Lanre

A child's daring mind
Shines with brighter ideas
Nothing impossible beyond her reach

Copyright Ulma Taboada

Dreams fuel
Dedication and devotion do miracles
Determination reaches the goal.

Copyright Pragyan Parimita Nanda

I could coal up the mines
Turn on the lights
No physics no mechanics beats the sun and the moon

Copyright Oiray J.Kings

Sun rays falling on the man's hand
Heralding hope
In lives on God's land!

Copyright Ritu Kamra Kumar

The sunrise caught
Between my fingers
Paints happiness in soul

Copyright Silviya Veselinova

The rays of the sun
Lies upon my palm
Hope never dies

Copyright Lucy A. mandala

The love of God never ceases
Even with littlest of hope
He squeezes.

Copyright Nathaniel D. Cruz

Each morning in an invitation
To heed God's call for influencers
To godly life.

Copyright Loreta C Bande

Dazzling sunrise
Radiant daylight focus
Shafts of beam ray shine

Copyright Daniel Miltz

Soft rays of sunshine
At start of the day
Warm every hearts all the way!

Copyright Rhodora Garcia-Medina

When I have the sun to hold
Who needs gold?
Sunshine is my world

Copyright Vijaya Sarmah

Fingers waded in sunrays
Eternal light showers
Defeated darkness

Copyright Sihem Cherif

Rays of hope are visible,
They teach, even the
Sun is within our reach!

Copyright Gopal Sinha

Many blessings like this,
Always as you wish,
So that nothing
You'll miss.

Copyright Kenneth Munene

Reaching for the sun
A splash of gold
To illuminate my world

Copyright Nandita De

I feel the
Warmth of this
Rays feeling you

Copyright Uzo Nwamara

New day dawns
Offers fresh start
Grasp opportunity

Copyright Margaret Karim

A fistful of sunlight I collect
To bathe in delight
Forget my plight.

Copyright Chandra Sekhar Batabyal

The sun rises up silently
Between my fingertips I see
Perceived much its heat...

Copyright Zenaida Laragan Taloza

Catching past love
To catch new one
Catching is not matching.

Copyright Amb Maid Čorbić

You can say goodbye to the land
But never...
To the Sun

Copyright Ronel David

You cannot touch the sun...
Yet you feel it...
The Same As we Love

Copyright The Ono

Reaching for the sun
It slips
Right through my fingers

Copyright Pamela Tennant

The beams of light sifting through
Fanning past the fingers like shafts to the world
Are the only hope we have got at heart

Copyright OiRay Jay

Dawn ushers golden light of
Positivity, energy and blessings
Soak in nature's opulence.

Copyright Anjana Prasad

The warm touch of the sun's light
Hopes feels inside
God dwells in us.

Copyright Janet Licudo

Her Hope:
A glimpse of sunshine
After the darkest night
Copyright Alvin Agena Andino

It’s in your hands
To give the warmth love to people
Like the sun

Copyright Ency Bearis

Golden rays scattered
Blessings shower on my palms
New morning hopes.

Copyright Pragyan Parimita Nanda

Rays penetrates through the hole.
Sparkling through as it splash the floor.
I elongate my hands towards the door...

Copyright Yassin Okinyi

The emerging warmth from
The sun rays was a source
Of energy for performances

*Copyrigh*t Okoi Amadiowei Jacob

If you will ever go
Leave our benignant moment
If you will ever go

Copyright Ogundijo Segun Daniel

Fluffs of sunset rays
Fondle at tips of my memory,
Where beauty, gently sways!

Copyright Obingo Wesonga

The sunshine spreading...
On my fingertips...
Brings in new hope and aspirations...

Copyright Madhuri Kulkarni

Welcome to the new day
Capturing the sun ray
Keeping journey towards my destiny

Copyright Halima Khan

Come running here
To catch a handful of sunray
To start a new life.

Copyright Prashanta Kumar Samanta

A journey to cherish
With the sun's company
Or is it a warning?

Copyright Amrita Mallik

Sun is in my control
With sheer will power
The universe I conquer

Copyright Sudha Dixit

Holding sunrays in my palm
Soothe my soul calm
In the journey of life

Copyright Princess Lubna

Love's, sunshine spreads
Warmth, joy’s, hope’s, rays radiate daily
Sunrise paints, world, glows, happily.

Copyright Vinod Singh

With my woebegone hand
Welcomes the new dawn
To endure every grain of sand.

Copyright Ben-Hur Sistoso

Love touches everything
Leaves nothing to complain
Can enter every crevice of life.

Copyright Ramesh Chandra Pradhani

The ray of sun
To show all hopeful sights
For the winning sigh!

Copyright S Afrose

Divine light ,limitless and omnipotent
Is visible even through
One’s invincible unawareness's obscurity.

Sunrise touches the ground so soulful
Seas can see
Why not humans feel the pleasure

Infinite in nature
We barely understand
We are but a grain of sand.

Copyright Vee Barnes

You in the sky with stars,
it shines brighter,
than the others.

Copyright Ollga Farmacistja

reminiscing our night talks
Melodious rhyme singing
Thrill the whole soul

Copyright Yanita Asikasari

I dream of you tonight
With you holding me tight
Under the moonlight

Copyright Bernadette Lejarde

I live beyond the stars...
My life no more scars...
As Beauty it prevails...

Copyright Tha Ono

Like the stars on a dark night
You stand by me, my knight
Until day shines our next page

Copyright Taferi M. Simon

Twinkling stars smile and
The moon shines bright light
Filling peace and bliss.

Copyright Gatot Malaisianto

Form of consistent blasphemy,
Quiet propriety
Seldom cacophony,

Copyright Manmohan Rajbanshi

The only lonely star
Shines so bright with a scar
Betrayal crushed me apart.

Copyright Priti Dhopte

The sky full of stars
Erasing the darkness
Hope shines brighter

Copyright Pragyan Parimita Nanda

A wish upon a star is optimism
Let fate be kind
From wisdom sky

Copyright Ency Bearis

As the stars brightly shining,
You and I together
Lives happily ever after.

Copyright Edmon Libres

Stars in night
Splendid nature calls
For first awakening

Copyright Maid Čorbić

Star lit ambience
Cocoons lovers
Fosters romance

Copyright Margaret *Karim*

This is me... that is you...
She showed the stars...
Saying... I love you...

Copyright Madhuri Kulkarni

Counting memories abound
Sensing a nostalgic thrill at night
A stellar cacophony

Copyright Mir Samsul Haque

Myriad of dreams
Gleaming like stars
In the glittering, glamorous eve

Copyright Seema Sharma

Gazing at the stars, let's cast a wish
May our relationship,
Never lose luster

Copyright Suveera Bellary Kusnur

Dazzling my desires
Upon inky night sky
Get up! Go stellar

Copyright Nishat Jabeen

Like the stars that shine
Let us be the light
To brighten other's life...

Copyright Ning Gaspi Gaton

As we dream together
Let us both reaching up
The millions of stars above.

Copyright Gloria A. Yu

Our love rekindles when we're together
It shines like the bright stars...
Precious time!

Copyright Marissa P. Esmeralda

Glittering like diamonds in the sky
Dreams to reach the impossible
Twinkling stars...

Copyright Lucy A. Mendiola

Together counting blessings
Our fingers delicately touching
Each shining star
Life of pure bliss!

Copyright Princess Lubna

In the sky of my mind
The star of love had risen
Mercifully no one responded.

Copyright Palash Baran Das

A wish in the sky
Gazillions of dream
My countless fantasy.

Copyright Vicente A. Valdez Jr.

Sometimes even pragmatic lovers
Dare to dream upon the stars
On a magical night.

Copyright Loreta C Bande

New love found is sweet,
Killing every time you meet
Like sparkling stars go lit.

Copyright Rhodora Garcia-Medina

Two diamonds in the sky,
Shining like stars up high,
We'll never say goodbye.

Copyright Kenneth Munene

A placebo wish I make,
To soothe and heal me,
Before it disappears.

Copyright Amrita Mallik

Gleaming stars of the night,
Are star witnesses
To our love and endless promises.

Copyright Ben-Hur Sistoso

I choose that star for you.
Your choice mine not,
Love only likewise.

Copyright Maria Elvira Fernandes Correia

Darling, go to the sky
We will stay like the stars
Bidding everyone goodbye.

Copyright Prashanta Kumar Samanta

Twinkling stars at night
Remind us of all those loved ones,
We had lost.

Copyright Anu Gupta

Stars smiling above
In the dark ambience of the sky
Positive notes they proclaim.

Copyright Chandra Sekhar Batabyal

When there is no moon,
The stars show us
The right path to follow.

Copyright Gopal Sinha

Astrologers, searching for
Somewhere by divine directive
Through the brightest Star in the sky

Copyright Okoi Amadiowei Jacob

Share with me the stories
Written in the stars
That filled you,
With wonder

Copyright Shamain Simeon

Like the shining sequins
On a dark cloak, are sewn
Stars of my desires

Copyright Sudha Dixit

Romance of the starlight
Hearts pounding in unison
Love stealthily creeping in

Copyright Nandita De

Wish I chance upon
A shooting star
That grants my longings and desire.

Copyright Sujata Dash

Star dancers you and I
Side by side way up high
Under the night sky.

Copyright Pamela Tennant

Just little space observed
In lonely psyche paves
Starry vast space-
Absolute nothingness's flooding

Copyright Dr Amiya Rout

Oh, stars guide my love,
Groping life's uncertain nights,
Hold our hands to blissfulness.

Copyright Marvin Marcelino

Stellar skies, guiding light
Dazzling in darkest night
Open arms for grace infinite.

Copyright Anjana Prasad

Angels of the sky
Stars kissing earth-
Pleasing to mind's eye!

Copyright Ritu Kamra Kumar

Every twinkling star
Seems to tell a tale
Of a moment that elapsed.

Copyright Kirti V

To Moon, stars,
See twinkles
For dear ones sighing, on earth.

Copyright Vinod Singh

That brightest star
A good omen for us
May our love continue forever?

Copyright Kishor Kumar Mishra

Underneath a sky full of stars
A man's heart
Should not be in despair

Copyright Vijaya Sarmah

Millions of stars:
Clear yet unreachable
Like our dreams

Copyright Alvin Agena Andino

Among the countless dreams
Hanging in the sky
My star will shines so bright.

Copyright Dolo Rez

Darkness may overshadow the world
Nothing can outshine love
When two hearts remain allured.

Copyright Liege Lord Lanre

In the vastness of God's firmament
I'm only a speck of dust;
God's wisdom.

Copyright Medy Villapando

Under the skies,
Twinkling stars witness our eternal love,
Carrying million dreams, we sleep!

Copyright Amrita Lahiri Bhattacharya

My Oath.
Unto the smiling moon
I oath to show my love
And pour my heart

Copyright Kerchia Festus Terlumun

Under the wing of darkness
Millions of stars
Playing hide and seek

Copyright Mafizuddin Chowdhury

These the stars, rule our lives
Deciding fates
Even, who'd be, man and wife

Copyright Ronel David

November

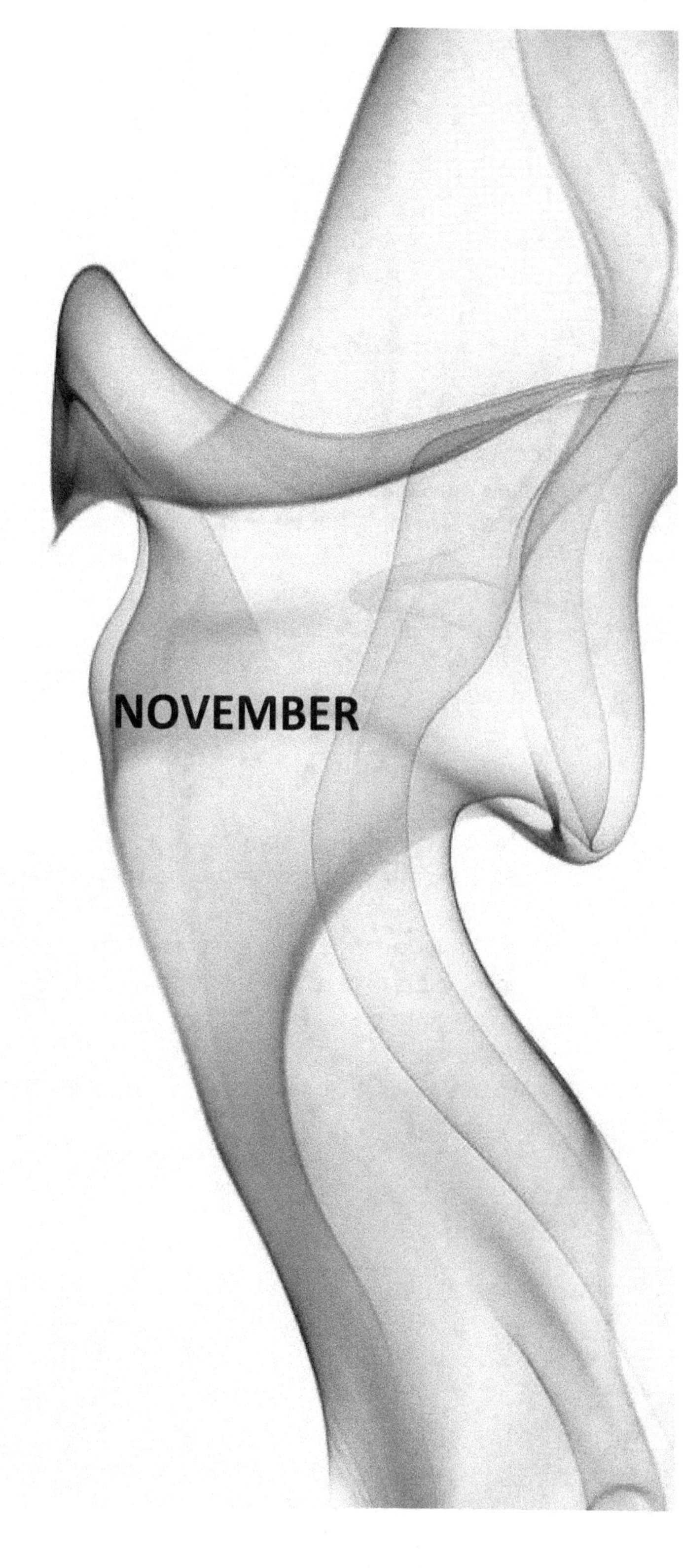
NOVEMBER

HELLO TO NOVEMBER...

Whole past months
Battling with feelings
With dry emotions
Heart mixed with tears

With unhealed words
Lost the lines of rhyming
To ink the isolation
May this November cherish my mood?

Dear November, color up the sky
With multicolored rainbow
That light up the hearts of innocents
Oh!! November have a shower filled with gold pennies

To turn the "rags" "into" "clothes"
Tune the song of Nightingale
To heal the wounds of poor souls
Dear! November bring us happiness with hot coffee

To feel the romantic for the secret lovers
Shed droplets of love to the barren land
Oh ! November, erase the horror word "war"
May the world light up their faces as candles
With the dawn of November with tons of everlasting dreams...

Copyright Dimithri Wijerathna
Sri Lanka

LOVE STORY LINES IN NOVEMBER

Tonight I will tell the secret of love
Love has changed my way
When November comes with sweet smile
Filling the days with gladness
Time really passes by so fast
November calls me so friendly
I don't know it is warm greeting or sorrow
I must keep strong to face what will happen
November tells the happy story behind the rain
Sunset and darkens go and return
I don't care about it
I must live, laugh and love in November
Loneliness in the eyes has said good bye
November brings me to enjoy sunset
The beauty of sunset forces me
Craving the words to say I love you
Rain, love and yearning colors the sky of November
Let's finish our love story lines
The wind is jealous with me
And rain is the last our love story
I have written the spring of love in the beauty of November
I am powerless to express true love
November has hurt my feeling
Like an arrow flies to hit my heart
One has won to reach your love

Indonesia

NOVEMBER

Nearing the final month of the year
Opened my windows November was here
Velvety skies that mirrored the sun,
Early reminders of what's set to come.

Movement of seasons were well underway
Blistering heat waves coming our way
Early reminders that Christmas was near
Righteous and joyful at this time of year.

Ready for flip flops and sunscreen galore.
Every beach brimming, we head to the shore
Bathers on ready, towels and our hats
Melting of ice creams, beach balls and bats.

Everyone splashing trying to keep cool
Very red bodies from acting the fool.
Olive brown skin soon set to appear
Now it has reached this time of year.

Not quite summer yet it's on its way
Only the start of what's set to stay.
Velvety skies and crystal clear waves
Everyone eager exploring the caves.

Mention of soft serve, kids will appear
Bubbly and joyful at this time of year.
Everyone chilling down by the shore
Ready to splash and cool down some more

Raising the flags for safe swim and play
Earlier sunrises to stretch out the day
Burning bare feet on piping hot sand
Mention of surfing there'll be one at hand

Enjoying the evening a day full of fun
Velvety waters reflecting the sun
Only the start of what's set to stay
November it brings a much brighter day.

FABULOUS NOVEMBER

November, a month of splendor,
I crave for the month ever.
Fluffy white clouds float across the sky lazy,
After raining so long they are drowsy .

Dew drops shine like beads of diamond on the tips of grass,
A necklace formed by morning sun's loving gleams.
White kasha flowers nod their heads in the morning breeze in glee,
A poet can't but be lost in their spree.

Lotuses unfurl petals one by one by the kiss of sun ray,
I stand for hours to see the heavenly splendor by the pond in gay.
Sheuli flowers bloom in lakhs in the evening in my court yard,
A sweet persistent smell comes pouring in the Zephyr to enliven nerves jaded.

After a night's merriment the flowers fall flat on the ground at dawn,
I care to collect them in a pot every morn.
A sweet note rings through the air and the sky,
Only the Bengali heart can feel that high.

It echoes the great advent of their festival,
Waiting for mother Durga's arrival...
Autumn's magic at work to make the maple leaves fall,
For new leaves to adore nature's hall.

Autumn's bird sing sweet notes in the bushes,
Nature's orchestra never misses.
Nice to boat in the river after the rain,
Waves in the river push the boat without refrain.

Hilsa fishes swim on the water surface,
Silvery look they flash to the eyes 'grace.
Ignorant, they are soon to be netted by fishers,
To be sold for palatable dishes at homes.

Copyright Chandra Sekhar Batabyal
India.

THE LAST LEAVES HAVE FALLEN,

And the ground is bright and beautiful
And colourful with the quilt of leaves;
There is a chill in the air
And frost on the grass,
November has arrived and there is a thrill in the air.
November the month of festive anticipation,
The month of shorter days,
And longer nights,
The month of preparation,
The month of cleaning up
For the festive season.
November, the month of romance,
The month of walking
Under cold starry skies,
The month of warm embraces,
And passionate kisses.
November, the month of bright, twinkling lights,
Every house, every church, every tree is glowing,
Everywhere you can hear sweet voices singing
And practicing Christmas carols,
November, the most soothing month,
Filling the heart and soul with peace
And love and joy.
Ah! Splendid November,
You are such a precious treasure,
You bring us such glorious pleasure.

PENULTIMATE MONTH OF THE YEAR

Ok, the great
Cheerful month of November
Being outside
Searching for experience
The hints of winter
Consume the space
Brilliant winter birds
Animals all over the place
With cold
And blanketed
Days to come
We end up playing
Outside in abundance
Both tomfoolery and useful
We yell with merriment
That gives invited quietness
As the sun's weak effort
To heat the November air
At the ground surface
It starts to
Ascend and cool
As there are yet
A couple of heavenly
Sprouts all over
O' as pre-winter coals
Move forward
A colder time of year punch
Creeps into the chill feeling
As the last exit
Whilst' we think
That it is wonderful
Our faculties' blossom

NOVEMBER OF THE GLORY

On November 28, One Thousand Nine Hundred Twelve
Lightning in Shkrepëtina, the sky opened, the clouds disappeared

Albanians from all over Albania
In Vlore they raised a legend.
The world is listening from side to side
the leader of the two lions
Ismail Qemal Bej Vlora
Isa Boletin the eagles.
29 - the forty four
back in the history
Eagles wiped out fascism
in red and black November.
You are the November of pride
chilled out two stories
It's the flag two proud
it is also the fight for freedom.
November you are a second spring
The begonia and lily are blooming
They didn't grow up with water
They grew up with blood clots.
Take it, a branch of begonia
Blood drips, it drips from the hands
Blood of the boys of liberty
And the old man Qemal Vlora's.

NOVEMBER WINDS BLOW

Rich glowing colours
Crisp autumn day
Summer long forgotten
Winter on the way
We walked in the park
Crackle of leaves
Watched their joyful dance
In a sudden breeze
Blue skies transformed
Mesmeric ease
Swollen clouds appeared
Intent on release
Rain fell
Fierce pitter patter
Laughing, hand in hand
We ran for cover
Canopy of trees
Scented shelter
Breathed deeply
Fragrance of Nature
Shower soon over
Wispy sun shimmered
Water diamonds twinkled
Foliage glimmered
Love in our hearts
Faces aglow
Still recall your smile
As November winds blow

MIRROR NOVEMBER

Activating personal protection in November,
With a mystical power of the potent eleven,
Acting as a catalyst setting in motion,
New life and new beginnings,
Realign, re-focus, and re-grow your strength,
Rest assured by the sacred warrior,
Celebrate your home, family and friends,
Amplify your prayers o'er collective bounty,
Acknowledge slowing down for a greater renewal,
Transition from the autumnal harvest to the
degenerative winter,
And so you must respond positively,
To the change, and adapt in a better way,
For a fruitful life ahead,
In this karmic month, be prepared,
For all your good and bad deeds,
For its fast catching up with your life,
A month also for celebrations and excited energy,
Some adieus are meant to be welcomed,
Some doors need to be shut,
And, some good need to be yanked,
In this mirror month, be a little more mindful,
Of your good conduct and right behavior,
Be open to awakening, action and alertness,
And adopt, discretion, generosity and compassion,
You'll have nothing to be afraid of,
As you breezily sail through the transition.

RUMINATION IN NOVEMBER

As summer gone, enter congenial climate
Much I have thought with advent of autumn
With breathe of autumn ambiance to feel
And the gentle wind, temperate atmosphere

Indeed conducive clime of the year
With great fruition to think about
Along with leaves changed to vibrant hues
The colorful surroundings upon my view

Gives comfort, healthful to psych
Much I have thought of chain of events
As the earth's facet to russet leaves color
And some leaves in gold tints to behold

Much I like with atmosphere gives splendor
But within September to October leaves falling
Maybe forlorn figures at the town of trees
I think it's just Mother Nature's ephemeral touch
Yet, autumn usher's the November affair

N oticeably the Autumn moment still within
O h, it's November month with great scenario
V ividly colorful leaves any which way to luv
E ven the ground, polychromatic everywhere
M isty days, bone-chilling feeling momentum
B ecause of the shivery atmosphere to absorb
E re night, foggy shroud 'til morning come
R ationale to November phase, then to winter

N ovember, November my forethought upon
O f the phenomena, and point of view also
V ibrating in good rhythm like in leitmotiv
E xpecting quite soon the holy, jolly songs to be
M erry month, and holidays thusly to transform
B ut within November Thanksgiving is superb
E thical act, giving thanks to blessings thence
R umination by me the modes of November

KARMA

Fifteen the date of my birth...
November the month that brought me into the world to challenge my worth...
Steps and strides day by day abide ...
Knowing I am that of a water sign...
A Scorpio is me that is true...
For this makes me resilient so I can float above days of gloom...
November always a month of wonder...
A blessing to those who understand true karma...
For the drama may bring bitter moments...
Like November brings Thanksgiving so bitter sweet...
Karma brings the just desserts to every meal...
Gray November days can lead to January days of hope...
Forgiving but never forgetting the moments that left you for broke...
Cracks and torn...
You will always remain whole...
You may see days of red...
Wishes and dreams stolen ...
Midst of the fall season...
November always gives you a reason...
A reason to stand...
Strength to reserve your passion...
As leaves turn for a future to be reborn...
Karma steals your tears so you may find your smile today and beyond...
Running through the weeks fifty two ...
Of days three hundred and sixty five with six as a bonus...
You can always tell November is upon us...
For life remembered on the first and of the second...

Celebration of life which upon earth walked has ended...
For Karma served better than revenge for those souls she defend...
November rains are not strange ...
Birth no matter the ticks of the clock...
Gives each soul that November luck...
Time may go...
November flows...
Karma reigns even if she may be slow...
Remember always my November child...
Always forfeit your pride...
When karma is at your side...
Your glow shall not be gone as your countenance will always be fitted with a smile...

Copyright Tha Ono

NOVEMBER

Not only is it simply a month with eleven as its number
It beholds and simultaneously unfolds many thrills in its hamper
Its arrival brings with itself a little chill
Snowfall begins to knock uphill
Festivities begin to gather in a flock
Everyone dresses up to look presentable and rock
Sequential events mark the festivities
Irrespective of caste, creed and racial disparity
Ebullient bursts of energy and enthusiasm
Bountiful jubilations create atmosphere of recreation
For me this month is even more special
As God has chosen it for my birth coincidental
To wait for its arrival, there is a tickle in my nerves
So my liking above the rest, is this month definitely deserves
No sooner it arrives
I wish that it may long thrive
It brings out the naughty child within me
Wanting all intelligence of middle age to flee
Carrying me on the wings of fantasy
This month gifts me with countless bliss in bounty
Despite being a little chilly, its arrival gives me tempting warmth
So comforting to my pounding and unrest heart
Every year this month gives me the realization
That life is an event and celebration
Each moment is to be put to optimum use
Lest one may left with a never ending regret to remain infused

ODE TO NOVEMBER

Oh! Dear November
You come in tips and toes
With a sweet smile on your lips
Filling the days with beauty, happiness
All the months passed away
November hugs me with love
It gently touches my heart.

November takes me to see
The beauty that matured around the world
Sometimes it takes me far far away
Behind the beautiful seashore
To watch the waves that rise and fall
The life of joy and sorrow
As evening falls
November brings me the enjoyment of Sunset

The beauty of sunset on the sea
Which forces me to fill my
Hearts with words of joy and love
I simply smile and say to November
'Oh! I love you very much'
Oh!dear November
You give birth to exquisite beauty to
My Garden with colourful roses, flowers

The spring of love emerges
In the garden of beauty of November.
November has turned my garden into Paradise
That cannot be expressed in words.

November
Let your face shine with beauty and smile
Swathe your lips with kind words of joy
Fill your souls with love
That will touch my heart with happiness

Copyright Sharmistha Das

NENTORI

Vjeshta e trete eshte duke ardhur
me gjethe te rena si gjithemone.
Eshte fundi i nje stine qe fort e dua ,
se vjeshta i ka te gjitha per ta dashur.
Ne pyllin e dendur me drure gjithandej,
po fryn ere cmendur se vjeshta po vjen.
E jeshilta e bukur nuk duket gjekund,
u xhvesh i tere pylli nga era tund e shkund.
I mahnitshem gjelberimi sic ishte u zhduk.
Skeletin e pyllit vec era lekund.
Çme vajtoka i mjeri ashtu mbytur sot.
I ka ikur gjithecka qe donte aq fort.
Vjeshta pikon e tera perjashta
e rruga eshte plot trishtim,
ndoshta nga ikja e gjetheve
apo nga dicka tjeter,
qe ngjan me ikje pa kthim.

Copyright Ollga Farmacistja

MONTH CALLED NOVEMBER

Months were not there when God was creating the world
It started in a day, and from days unto weeks, and weeks
At then there were no months in numbering of hours in life
Yet mortal moment continues to increase in measurement
Then a month was born when Adam was one month in life
Since then, month after month are here with us in existence
Starting with January, the first child of the year, as it grows
Gradually to February, March, April, May and June in timing
Which becomes the First Half of the Year before it moves on
From July to August to September to October to November to
December, being the Last Daughter of every Year in mortality
Whenever the year begins its journey from days to weeks and
From weeks to months and from months to termination of time
It comes with fresh features such as winter, spring, autumn and
Summer for which each comes with its benefits and deficiencies
November, the penultimate month of every year is significant as

It serves as a period of preparation in waiting for the birth of its
Last Daughter which is nobly known as December, a Daughter of Delight as humanity rejoices for the grace of being alive till date
In November, everybody is aptly active in preparing for December
Both humanity and spirits are anxious to end it up successfully
We are once getting close to November hence are preparing for
The last daughter of the year which is known as sister December
When it is November, the land is dry as the wind is whistling
The grasses are grey but the flowers are flourishing very well
The beasts are busy, and mammals are many, with fishes full
When it is November, Mom and Dad will buy many new clothes
For themselves, and for us. We are happy, highly happy in our home
All are happy in waiting for Christmas, for Rice and Stew, in our home

Copyright Okoi Amadiowei Jacob

THE AUTUMN FALL IN JAPAN

How beautiful it is to view...
The autumn in Japan...
The spectacular hues mesmerizes the hearts of the onlookers...
The Maple and the Gingko trees...
Paint the gardens in gold and crimson...
They are sparkling in the November sun...
The vibrant red, yellow and orange leaves...
Signal the entry of autumn fall...
In September they start shedding dead leaves...
October passes... But in November...
They are at their peak...
The fall brings in romantic tones... with a tinge of sadness attached to them...
Young couples take outdoor walks. Hand in hand...
Over the carpet of vivid hues...
Savoring the season...
Mountains in Hokkaido start changing their colours in late October...
Following suit are the leaves by November...
While "SAKURA" is to spring
"MOMIJI-GARI" is to autumn...
Momiji meaning red leaves...
Gari is hunting of them...
Let's explore the country of Japan...
And enjoy the hues of all seasons...

Copyright Madhuri Kulkarni

THE TASTE OF FIRST LOVE

Smiling on the summer wind.
The vast world feels comforting.
Sending countless memories
My heart longs for love and happiness.

The season witnessed the passing of time.
Where parting and departing savor the chilly chime.
To break the broken silence of time.
In the snow of dreams, will your heart be still mine?

The hearts still remember each other.
Even the world is changing ever.
How does time pass so quickly?
How does the world change before me?

The rain added sorrow to the heart in pain.
The sound of rainfalls blends with her lament.
It's hard to depart from the one we love.
It's melancholy, dreadful, and sad.

Flower bloom and wilt as moment pass by.
Will you travel far and drift with the wind up high?
As the clouds meet the moon on a frosty night.
Will our love remain for eternal life?

The season tastes all the flavors of love.
The withering leaves start plunging out.
Who listens to the silent voice of the rain?
Whose hearts knows what she is missing?

How deep can love go?
Whose life will spend in a blow?
Can you come with me?
For the blissful journey, we can share each day.

Life is like an empty page.
Only the heart knows to browse its text.
Will your heart skip a beat, whenever you meet me?
Like how the bird finds its canopy in the leafless tree.

November is here.
Shall I let go of the memories or shall I waver?
The taste of first love is bitter and sweet.
As the falling petals showered down the earth.

November holds the stories of summer and spring.
Where happiness was experienced and mistakes were earned.
Where love and hate flavored the season.
Love is like a dream, enjoy it while it was in full bloom.

Copyright Janet Licudo

THE SEASON TREADS SOFTLY

Shorter days and longer nights
Less of fun more of sighs
Hello November!
I can sniff well
You have perched with your entourage
To rule and shine
The autumn sun
Amid fluffy frothy flakes of wandering white
Gaily plays a game of hide and seek
Peering through the clouds
It thoroughly enjoys its sojourn
Having shed their precious green ensembles
Bade farewell to the mellowed ones
Bare trees stand tall in defiance
Eagerly await new shoots and leaves
To fill landscapes with exuberance
Their longings to mend broken ties
Bear similar pattern to homo-sapiens
As we mortals dearly miss bygones
Crave for things of past
Let nostalgia wimple softly into the arena of life
The fall symbolizes a temporary halt
As rise after every fall is certain
Soon damp misty evenings will wean
Vistas of spring's undiluted bliss
Will paint the sky with an aura of gleam.

DAYS OF NOVEMBER

Nippy evening's cold long nights
Warm quilts, under starry lights
Mother's hot spicy meals
Come November, season of winter dreams and misty mornings

Cupful's of flavored tea
Books to read, sitting in cozy balconies
Or lie on a quiet beach
Watching the lazy winter sea

A lone country boat, rocking gently in the waves
Happy boatman weaving fishing nets
Mild, moderate November days
No winter harshness, nor summer's fiery blaze

Only the scent of receding autumn still lingers on the afternoon sun
In the backyard granaries and the barns.
Pruned rose bushes, mowed lawns in every house
Harvested fields with left out stalks of corn

The scent of burnt wood in the air
Feathered friends croon on the old clock tower
Fall of leaves, mist laden trees
Winter whispers on neon lit streets

Old folks sit around warm bonfire, reminiscing nostalgic yesteryears
Carefree youngsters strum the guitar
Hum old country songs, with husky voice
November days, let us rejoice, before December's bitter
Cold crack the bones.

MISS NOVEMBER

November brings back sweet sad memories of Miss November,
This impossibly beautiful girl i met on the Net in September.
To say i miss November is an understatement,
Though our long distance fling lasted up to December, it was like i had known the girl all my life and within a month, by October, words like "wife" and "for life" were becoming easier to say and pronounce.
To my utter disappointment Miss November decided to stand me up in December. I went to the airport to wait for her, roses in hand, blooms of pure love in my heart, dreams of deriving a family from first principles in my head, but alas, the plane off-loaded everything else, except Miss November.
I was so devastated i had to lean on a fire tender, and when i fainted some pretty nurse had to render CPR, her mouth to mouth so sweet i thought Miss November had finally arrived.
From that day in December i went into depression right up to November the following year, yearning for my Miss November, sitting round a dead fire full of ambers, sometimes in anger, sometimes like an angler, trying to fish out where i had failed.
Every November i remember Miss November and I miss Miss November every November.

NOVEMBER HUES

Emotions burgeon in great deal
In the month of November
Myriad of hues greet us
In our hitherto 'barren life'
Happiness proliferates
In abundance
As that the downpour
Drenches the parched land
And satiates the environment~
Hail, I hail thee!
November, thou art my kind of month~
In thy presence
I want to mingle myself
In fluorescent colours
Quenching all my desires
Blossoming as flowers
Recovering my faded beauty
I want to be one to one
With the scented air
That is felt in the clime
Rejuvenating my all numb spirits~
A palpable appeal
Of mild coolness
O, I feel~
As though
Winter seems standing
At the threshold
When air kisses me on my forehead
An exuberance, a bliss it feels!
Such enchantment
O November, thou create
This heart sings a melodious song

And it keeps wafting
Throughout the month
Like a phoenix
My expired spirits
Are desirous of taking rebirth
Nipping the mundanely in the bud
And relive this life each moment~
I want resurrection!
Wish November to live
Till eternity and beyond!

IT'S THE MONTH BEFORE DECEMBER

It's the month before December,
It has many wonderful things to remember,

It precedes the month of Christmas,
When people are about to start holidays,

When it's the beginning of festive season,
People are booking for the next vacation,

The weather is usually warm,
All around like a beautiful dream,

It's the start of celebrations,
Certain events without speculations,

We hold parties for our achievements,
We want to forget all the disappointments,

It reminds us that life is a journey,
At this time people spend a lot of money,

Schools are about to be closed,
Coming this far in the year feeling blessed,

It will be a New Year count down soon,
It's like having gone round the moon,

People look at what they have accomplished,
Looking for whatever to adjust before year is finished,

There's plenty of harvest,
There's more than enough to feast,

Everyone is in a happy mood,
You can see it in the neighborhood,

People can plan for New Year resolutions,
After overcoming many challenging situations.

NOVEMBER IS KNOCKING ON THE DOOR

November is knocking on the door
It carries colorful leaves and sadness,
Gone is the love on the bench,
The birds flew south.
The mists descended on the fields
The wind plays with the yellow leaves,
No butterflies, no flowers
Chest pain is pressing.
November is here
Extends invisible hands in winter,
The warmth of love disappeared in sleep
And I console myself,
A new November will come, a chance
Don't worry, I give you my love, my soul...

GATHER THE LEAVES AND STORE AWAY

Autumn Leaves
Giving up as time passed by
Nearing the end
As winter approaches;
Ready to cover the earth
In its bridal gear
And a coat to the trees that will shiver.
Gathering the leaves
Each:
'A promise never fulfilled,
A dream never realized,
A wound left open,
A heart left broken,
A pain still hurting,
A song never sang,
A word never said,
A sin never stopped,
A stranger never spoken to,
A friend never made,
A time wasted away'
Into a bag
Ready throw away

Or
Into an art piece
Ready to be made
November, November
A month that reminds one to wake up
As the day of the Son approaches,
Reminding all to wear the gear of faith,
As another year is about to open
With uncertainty.
Store away the leaves
To prepare for the cold
That passes the north.

FRAGRANCE OF HOPE!

I have wondered;
Been petrified
To the yoke,
About life, about own
Self: how on the pebbled
Pathways I trudged,
I managed to insist
This feeble feet controlled?
That fate, is pegged
On keeping trying,
On keeping sniff of perfume
Of hope to my faith,
Regardless!
I have wondered;
Been mystified
To my insides,
How like a luminous flash,
That time ebbs and
Freezes on stillborn
Dreams, nipping in bud?
How, against odds, have I
Kept my head held high
And deep in rioting
Headwinds? How have I
Kept faith on empty
Palms? How, I kept open
The eye of my heart
Even when full-color
Of my being, faded?
How, like, an eel,
Have I slithered
Passed thorns on

My pebbled path;
And left on it
An inspiring line
In its Psalms of hope:
Never fade, before you ace!
A soul of social grace!
Life is wonder beholden;
A magic of good
Anticipation, what more
On its legacy, than perseverance
To its unpredictability,
Where hate mocks love
And justice is pinned
On the mat of power,
Tagged on this floating
Bitter, sour world?
But, like a liman...
A sweet fragrance off
Embers of toil,
I am a good thought,
That took long to materialize;
A loving thought,
In a night of a soul!

Copyright Obingo Wesonga

FAT OF AUTUMN

From the deciduous
Golden-brown teeth of green wild,
Wafted in dry breeze of eminent
Autumn, saluting the
Burning yoke of the sun,
I open my two eyes, to thy site!
November: the harvest month!
As you beg with a knock
On this wide entrant door,
As you dye and fold leaves
To a crunch, as you host
A harvest to baskets of
Abundance, let hope, too,
Come tied, but on your tongue.
That when the autumn winds
Shall swish and flow from faunal
Overwhelmed ground, let such winds
Carry blessings on their wings.
That when free fruits fall from
Matured passion trees, we shall
Collect and collet our love for them
Knowing these changes in leaves
And fruits, keeps the soil fertile,
Keeps the doctor away.
Autumn; oh, fruit of toil,
Amount us into one being, without sway!

Copyright Obingo Wesonga

THE CHILL IN THE AIR

I feel the chill in the air
It brings the scent of winter
Oppressing heat of summer
Is no more in atmosphere?

It was a very long wait
Autumn, spring and hot season
Had gone before this month, it's
Cozy for mystic reason

It's different in India
Not much colder or icy
As it's in other countries
It's more pleasant, as I see

The verdant leaves remain green
Not whither or become brown
Neither too hot or too cold
It brings glamour to my town

I hear birds chirping sweetly
Watch butterflies chirping
Nature's filled with happiness
Look at the peacocks dancing

It's such a joyful month, those
Playful days I remember,
That were so comfortable
I'm glad to greet November

NOVEMBER IS A WONDERFUL TIME

Autumn is a picturesque season:
Yellow leaves on the background of the blue sky,
On the hill, an autumn carpet of crimson fallen leaves,
Some trees have turned yellow,
Others are still green.

The sun illuminates part of the river,
Light, fluffy clouds are reflected in the river,
The river seems silvery.
Fallen leaves swirl in slow eddies.

A slender, golden, white birch glistens in the sun.
Autumn is beautiful, it's time for autumn weddings,
time for rest.
For newlyweds, autumn is considered one of the most
favorite seasons.
Autumn offers inexhaustible opportunities for creating
a bright, beautiful event.

Autumn wedding are announced to newlyweds warm
love, long relationships and a strong family.
A wedding in November will provide the young family
with wealth.
A wedding is one of the most beautiful and important
events in a person's life, especially a woman's.
It is in autumn that you want to warm yourself in the
arms of a loved one,

And the sun's rays are especially gentle and gentle.
Every woman dreams of love.
Love is a gift from God, not available to everyone.
You can't hide anything from love it illuminates the true nobility of the human soul.
This real, beautiful feeling makes people happy.

ONE NOVEMBER TO REMEMBER

Vivid memories in warmth I do hold
The time my grandson gave me
A maple leaf in orange and gold
His way to say love's colorful as fall can be.

I hugged him for what my cousin did
Back home...sprucing up graves with flowers
And praying for our dear departed
Lovingly as in the previous yesters.

On the eleventh, the Remembrance Day
The men of the house hanged their flag
For the armed forces who made poppies sway
Redder for peace to gain a swag.

My grandson's school calendar shows
World Kindness Day, hope for the young
To be shielded from bullying that slows
Self-esteem, the curse of words from sharp tongue.

November 12 for many a nation
With the glorious foliage an awareness
Of children's rights and education
A day to think of future togetherness.

As the red leaves fall on lawn and deck
Thanksgiving for graces and harvest
While we do inventories for reality check
November traipses by, loved and ready to rest

NOVEMBER SPEAKS

I arrive sixty one days before year end
For my annual stay in this world
Sky looks clear, also streams and rivers
Woods and gardens get filled with flowers.

Dawn stays beautiful, so also dusk
Morning and evening bring saffron look
Moon and stars perform in night sky
Orion, the hunter prominently stays.

Meteor showers occur in the sky
Leonids, Orionids, Taurids nearby
Andromedids, Phoenicids also shower
Men call them as 'shooting star'.

My thirty days stay are time of celebration
I bring some fairs, festivals and function
Autumn still continues its tenure on Earth
Wind gently brings winter's smooth touch.

Hard winter still remains at a distance
No frost, no snow to cover land mass
Wheat is planted in globe Northern
Vegetables ready to be reaped soon.

Thirty one days remain after my stay
December comes and I say good bye
Planning for a return in next year
I wait patiently in a new calendar.

Earth is beautiful, nice are all climates
Lovely surroundings, beautiful environments
Protect your environment, protect the Nature
Reduce grey hue, help growing Green Earth.

SONG OF NOVEMBER

The swallow's call-- it's time for
Feathers strong and a flight long
Gliding through mist and clouds
On a chilled November morn.

A voyage empyrean to down south
Formations close, not to stray
They fly on in a dance daring
To warmth of survival on their way.

A yearly ritual, fideltous utmost
The song of November, a travel through slumber
Arduous, relentless, they soar and flutter
Leaving behind the icy wind, tireless, on they lumber.

To a land of warm welcome
Thriving life in all splendour,
To the coziness of cheerful smile
And lakes blue with green fodder.

The November odyssey, laden with fantasy
Adventurous and tragic, the weak miss the magic
Flapping wings close in, any gap to fill in
A moving shadow of dotted triangles stays frantic.

November feeds the embers to a clarion call
To re- posture, restructure and change
Our journey's gear to tests severe
To re- route our dreams for an overhaul!

Swati Das

NOVEMBER TO REMEMBER

I...
What is spectacular about you, November?
That is something I have to remember
Hidden secrets and symbols need to unravel
An arrangement of weather from autumn to winter
Ephemeral time we need to embrace.
The dramatic backdrop starts to change in different hues
As the nighttime lengthens, daylight dims
A chance to gather strength as hibernal season follows the edge
Everything will change as the withered leaves start to fall
All will fall asleep in the dark frosty night.

II.
You are the bridge to a joyous season
After the candles lit all over the place
A short period of time someone I should remember
Or my mind would peril not to bless his soul.
Tomorrow after, a prelude to the holiday season
Yuletide carols starting to fill the air
Twinkling lights and lanterns lighted up the streets
Bring joy and thrills to every child's heart
This is the spirit of November air
The air of excitement and joyful gaiety

III
November, there is something in you to remember
Significant events that are long forgotten
A perfect time to renew the forsaken yore
A frown or smile is a big part to mend.
You are the penultimate month of the year
Never rushing, always waiting
Once you are here, we must relish each days
Filled it with memories to love and cherish
You stay for a month and we wait for a year
A continuous cycle for you and me.

Copyright Dolo Rez

OUR LAST NOVEMBER

It was an unusual morning
She's so silent, but full of spirit
Like an angel, she is staring
As I woke from our sleep

Her embraces makes me marvel
As if someone is about to leave
My lips, my eyes, she'll fondle
Wondering what she's trying to read

Squeezing her head on my chest
Like a baby to her mother
Saying nothing, only caress
Something seems to bother

It was November, a prelude
To a grief I never thought
Would there be an interlude
For sorrows that autumn brought

For those days were so ordinary
She's on her usual smiles
While I am in deep quandary
Why I feel her silent cries

Celebrations came and passed
No one can't see her pain
She too was laughing with us
Joys and sorrows seem the same

Then it came, after all pretenses
Time caught up with her acts
She left, drowning all my senses
My consent, she never asked

It was November, here again
May it over, and quick
'Twas her goodbye for heaven
Could've stopped her, but I blinked.

Copyright Nathaniel Cruz

AUTUMN FALL

The animals are scurrying about gathering their food to hibernate October is here.
Acorns, apples, pinecones and haystacks can be found everywhere.
You can't help but notice the cool, chilly, breezy, crisp air.
Time to harvest the pumpkins add cinnamon and nutmeg have your favorite brew.

Young lovers all cuddled up in a blanket enjoying the view.
The colorful leaves and trees of amber, crimson and auburn is a beauty to behold.
The sunlight upon it makes it glow becoming bright orange, yellow and gold.
This beautiful carpet of leaves scattered all over the ground.

Only in a few corners of the earth can this magnificent sight can be found.
Such wondrous and amazing phenomena of nature in all its glory oh what a sight.
To the dreamer, the artist, the photographer, the poet, the spectator... Autumn Fall is their utmost delight.

Oh to witness this
For the first time
Gives a feeling
So sublime

A feeling so fine
A creation of God
Nature's glory
For all the see
Animals and humanity
Rejoice

NOVEMBER

It's the eleventh month of the year
Sky looks blue, beautiful and clear.
Surface is dry and pleasant to move
For festivity November does approve.

Diwali, the popular festival of lights
Hindus spends a lot on crackers bright.
Buddhists in their temples and monasteries
Decorate and celebrate and have stories.

Light lamps and multi colored candles
Offer prayers with aromatic sandal.
Jains too don't give up the celebration
Liberation of Mahavir's soul and adoration.

Muslim community takes part and enjoy
Lighting up Dargahs with merriment and joy.
Family friendly nature reserves in November
Unites them all with the aromatic flavor.

The tiring sun moves fast to take a rest
The night searches a light blanket interest
Natural play areas are made crowded.
The days favor for tours and temporary shed.

Connect the children with natural environment.
To gather lovely experience for betterment
And the inspiration is entered to look after
And conservation of natural beauty hereafter.

Glamorous and exciting month forever
Enthusiastic every one and waits to devour.
Harvesting time comes up early
Farmers look at the grains pearly.

Store in the granary for the year
For calamities they don't fear.
Thanks giving to the almighty God
He brings smile minimizing his load.

THE MONTH OF NOVEMBER

Every year November comes quite late
Is November afraid to stand out in nature?
November is the eleventh month of the calendar
November is a nature's month full of special features

The field is full of ripening paddy
The smile on the farmer's face is the golden crops of the field
November gradually opens the door of winter
During the whole month no sweat is generated from the body

Neither cold nor warm conditions are very comfortable
Green leaves are falling one two three
The footpaths becomes a stage with colorful leaves
The mood of winter began to kiss the body

November is neither short nor big like May
Thirty days are getting shorter and the night is getting longer
There is not the least irony in falling rain
The hot clothes is started peeping

It has been locked in a box for ten months
The tangled life is very uncomfortable!
I like November very much
There is no discomfort of feeling hot on the body

There is no need to wear warm clothes because it is not cold
I feel free to walk around wearing a T-shirt
The month of change of season is very enjoyable
Dew buds on the tip of the grass are amazing!

In the dew I see myself in deep immersion
Would it be nice if November was the whole year?
November is unique in that it is a single month,
November.

NOVEMBER: A month of vows

November: An English Month covering maximum Indian 'Karta'
And minimum Indian 'Margasir ';
So pious for Indian inhabitants of this Earth, mother.
A month that contains Autumnal flavor and delicate winter –

The Clean blue with water-bereaved whitish clouds;
The clean blue with stars, planets and night;
Vast green with conceived Paddy fields
With water receding lotus finds with sun its rendezvous, sweet.

Even Cranes hesitate to pick up fishes in the water but what to talk of pious minds.
A month that rejoices cows and bullocks to be worshipped in their thatched sheds;
On shed walls are painted those domestic animals
And traditional agro -instruments' sketches.
A month that facilitates Devi Radar's feet to be worshipped

With devotion;
Reaffirms belief that in Rajas Purnima Lord Krishna had done his 'rasa'
With sixteen thousand gopis.
A month divine stories' impact makes one remember:
"Bada OSA" reminds about king Kratu cursed as leper;

Whose chaste wife could Destruction's God Appease?
Enabling her husband's disease cured;
For husband's good health, women observe this vow .
"Kanji Aanla Osa" reminds about merchant's wife losing seven sons;

Delivering her next babe at forest;
Getting her woe relaxed by "Sathi "Goddess;
By collecting from celebration's ground cooked rice;
And consequently getting her lost sons returned alive.
For protection of their offspring's women observe this vow.

"Manabasa Gurubara "/ first Thurs Day reminds about
Wealth-Goddess -graced untouchable lady;
Who mesmerized king and queen to be friendly with her;
Caste ridden heinous hierarchical ideas got rejected
And equality have had societal consent since then.

To get Goddess's favor, on Thursday women observe this vow
November: The confluence of 'Kartik ' and ' Margasir' month;
Every Indian waits for this month with earnest spiritual thirst.

IT'S, THAT TIME OF THE YEAR

It's, that time of the year
The start of the season of cheer
As winter looms close by
And autumn greets every street goodbye

Crispy sounds your steps relay
Crushing under, those leaves that lay
Dried and worn as they're blown on the streets
By the soft swaying winds as November we greet

The trees stand there, their nakedness all bare
Waiting for the snow to cover their despair
As we all prepare, for the season ahead
To brace the winter, knitting sweaters from woolen thread

The world over, across the globe
November comes, but different seasons it holds
The northern side gets ready to fight
Winters harsh, carrying longer nights

But the southern hemisphere, has a different song to sing
November comes in the midst of spring
Leaves, fresh and green, not brown and dead
Winter's far... still months ahead

And where I live, there are seasons few
Just these, winter, summer and monsoon too
Summer and monsoons, just heat and rainfall
The best but I feel, is winter, amongst them all
November is the month that's not cold, but yes
It is the start of winter nevertheless
It doesn't snow here, but it does get cold
As December comes, winter sets its hold

November, December, Jan, up to Feb
The pleasant of all, as thereon, winter begins to ebb
Although every season gives us something that we need
But I always long and wait, for November indeed

Copyright Ronel David

MAGICAL, MYSTICAL POWER OF NOVEMBER

Rains over, in months from August to September
Sun's strong, with cold winds blow, as climate changes in October
Winter is approaching at a fast speed in November
Autumn's crackling carpets, leaves fall from trees, in whirling, twirling showers.

Umbrella, cleaned, dried and stored away in trunks
November ushers in cool winter season, cool chilly winds flow
Warm clothes in sun to warm, in heat to get drunk
Cool morning, breeze tickles skin afternoon sun, makes me sleepy and skin glows.
Trees turn nude, leaves wither, die now winter approaches in bounds and leaps

Leaves fall, dancing in whirls, cool winds blow, saying bye to tree, and collect in heaps
Soon it's time for snow fall, animals go to hibernate
Birds ready to migrate to warmer climate, with lots of sun to feel warm, fly, liberated.
Birds are trees friends, sharing their joys, sorrows, it's difficult to say bye

Say, we fly to distant land, for warmth, food, we'll fly for miles
We are your loyal friends, can't beat, bear, snowy winters Giles
To survive harsh winter, is our goal, with God's given wings we'll fly to, save our souls.
Take care, enjoy snowy winters, charm purity, its softness and glow, O trees!

When we fly back it will be spring
Diary trees, you'll be dressed in green tender leaves, on branches we'll, hop, swing
Farewell, we go to distant lands, return when colourful flowers bloom in glee
God's circle of seasons, exists for a reason

Human life also follows, God's circle of seasons
November with its clash beauty, exists, as start of freezing season
Trees dressed in white snowy garbs, lovely snowy carpets, we tread, enjoy.
Light fires, spread warmth, hopes, as lovely memories flow

Makes us hold hands, eyes in love, happiness, togetherness glow
Way side fires decorate roads, eating peanuts, sharing news
Cups of tea, we drink, make merry, at winter gatherings, exchange views.
Winter's November magic, brings all close, sharing coats, blankets, snuggle in front of fireplace

With pets sitting at our feet, we share all, winters tasty treats.
Lovely festival, exchange of sweets Diwali, Halloween, we greet
All come together, exchange food, joy gifts, singing carols, on winter's frozen streets.

November, December, cold months of year as
temperature fall below zero
Days very short, nights are longer, we rest, to fight the
cold freezing weather low temperatures
Granny, mothers make all nutty sweets to promote
good health, give energy, all munch

Outdoor camp fires we light, play, sing dance together,
eat roasted onions, potatoes, nuts, enjoy goodies
crunch
Soon winter will get over, with New Year messages,
starts, and end of cold season.

Copyright Vinod Singh

A GUEST AT THE ELEVENTH HOUR

November is one month that takes great pleasure in dropping by to visit so late in the year. When November makes her grand entry, the people are expected to welcome her with a celebration galore. Because the people have become so much familiar with November, her luster has diminished. So no sweet familiar voice greets her ear on her arrival any more.
But November is. Such an unpredictable guest. The thirty days that she has to grace the year have some scattered surprises. The people however have come to view November as a damp and dreary month. A month of colorless sky and darker nights, of lusterless sun with no rays to soak up. A month when the trees lose their leaves and go bare... November is a month where most of the people have given up hope for the year. All because they have nothing to show for the past ten hectic months. They have failed to achieve their wishes for the year.
As November is the eleventh month, she represents the eleventh hour of the year. A much awaited miracle can happen even a second before November exits the year. When November comes your way again, do go about her with a sunny, cheerful and optimistic air.

KALEIDOSCOPE OF LOVE

PHILIA

Love comes in many forms
Truly a spectrum in every norm
A mother to her children
Selfless even to the brethren's

A father to his offspring's
Sacrifice up to the like of kings
The community as one
United in the flesh wherever you from

The legendary Cupid with bows
Two lovers see it beyond clouds
Venus the Greek Goddess
Inspires us to go away from sadness

The bible stated about the love of God
To all sinners, mercy from above
Unconditional one forgives totally
Whoever you are whole heartedly

Always keep in mind as a person
Love and heart has a reason
The reason itself cannot understand
Living a life full of hope in mind

Now gather here around
Fill our souls with loving hearts
Coming from all walks of life
No color, nationality and race can defy

PHANTASMAGORIA OF LOVE

Love makes
The world go around
And can sway many different ways
Everywhere you turn it shifts
Love moves mountains
Love, love, love
What is it?
Love is a fondness
Fills days with adoration new
Assaulting a psyche proud
When love floats in the breeze
It's an incredible feeling
With affection, keeps on delighting
Like pink petals on a rose
O' for all the year long
It's a day and night shout
Treasuring decorating ways
Adoration, emotion, devotion
All you need is love
The greatest gift of all
True love is a change
For the better
As love continues to grow
From dawn to dusk
It floats from head to toes

RAIN FORCES ME TO LOVE

There's no need to bring yearning
Staying by your side
Singing the song of rainbow
I know you still have broken heart
Your lover has left alone
Carving deep pain in the heart
I know the world where you live
It seems almost to ruin
I need you give me time
Telling poems of love you've written
When rainbow smiles for true love
Pouring freshness for spring of joy
Believe me! The wind has forced me
Entering the garden of love
It makes me to walk under the rain
Getting close to your heart
I know the words I speak
It's just like dust in the wind
Flying away without meaning
I hope you know what I feel
I have feeling more than just a friend
Carving the beauty of love for you
I need the wings of hope
Let my true love flow in your heart
I want to rest for a while
Looking at the beauty of smile
Before you close your tender eyes
Sleeping to hold night dream
I want to show you
How beautiful sunset is!
Spreading colorful light on the sky
Making the day so wonderful

Although, it will fall in the darkness
The beautiful sunset is yours
So is true love I will share
Decorating your life so warm and true
If you open the door of love
I will tie deep yearning
In the deepest lake of heart
I cannot live without your love.

Copyright Gatot Malaisianto

K.O.L.

High Infidelity
Time and Time again...
Question posed in more variety than poetry and prose...
What is Love???
Do you Love Me???
Is This Love for real???
Flowing through the rivers of time...
Sometimes parched upon rocks which make you smile...

A kaleidoscope of colours that blur your senses...
Filled with passion and high Infidelity when love releases...
Not on your brain...
Losing your mind...
Insanity lured by a cruel faith yet so divine...
Longing for what the heart wants...
Cannot feel or touch in a world of rush...
Your heart owned by another...

Your brain snaps in a moment of irony not held back...
Like a crumpled paper or broken mirror put back together...
Pieces may not be missing but you can still see the cracks...
What you pushed through cannot be undone...
What was once in darkness...?
Revealed by the ever shining sun...

For it may look beautiful for a moment in a true crime...
Soon dimmed because of colourful but even darker lies...
Illicit affairs or High Infidelity it screams so loudly...

Losing the only person who truly cares...
It is never done in error but moments arise...
Where you act on the kaleidoscope of love...
Making a journey you shall later despise...
Covering up what was done with lies...
Trying to fix the brokenness inside...
Sorry cannot repair the hurt...

A broken piano only playing sour notes...
Was the High Infidelity what it was worth???
Are you sorry you peered through that kaleidoscope???
Oh the west once won now forever lost...
A chokehold Cupid once held has been released...
Now cold dessert of Karma you now reap...
Please I do implore...
Do not follow the rose coloured kaleidoscope...
For you do not know what it has in store....

FILMING OF LOVE

One day ago
I am superb happy
I wish to seek love
Even when time is settled
I will stay so cool
Kaleidoscope of love
I wish to seek time
Love is best way
To be happiness
Forever I am happy
My time and my sense
World is amazing by my side
I will be so charity and full
Since I have deep sense of love
Forever I am happy now
My love and filming
I was supposed once again
To stay happy and cool
World is finished by my side
My entry is in the hearth

MEDLEY OF LOVE

A lifetime of love
Gathered around me
I am enveloped
In comforting energy
Pain recedes
Replaced by calm
Sense of peace
A welcome balm
My mind replays
Facets of emotion
Passion, intimacy
Tenderness, devotion
Romantic attachment
Paternal adoration
Amity, allegiance
Fraternal affection
Memories unite
Cloak my weary body
I am prepared
Final journey
Almost time to leave
I smile wistfully
Hard saying goodbye
To friends and family
I feel my mother's touch
She is ready to guide
Lifts my spirit
Carries it to the other side

ON WINGS TO PARADISE

When I look into your eyes,
I feel the weakness in my knees,

You see through to my heart,
Even though I don't know where to start,

We somehow find away,
And we are comfortable anyway,

You know where to touch,
There's no love button you cannot reach,

Everything becomes silent,
The room filled with your scent,

Giving me what I have been missing,
No details that are passing,

Because you know my body terrain so well,
And it's like saving me from hell,

I feel the fire with each kiss,
And we are lost in the bliss,

It's just the two of us in the house,
Free to do anything that we please,

You know how to excite my emotions,
As your hands move in hypnotizing motions,

You're the cure for my sickness,
You know how to give me happiness,

And our bodies find a rhythm,
You take me to heights I cannot fathom,

I am lifted on wings to paradise,
Everything you do is a sweet surprise,

We are lost in our own world,
What we feel cannot be described in one word,

The sweat and ragged bed is a beautiful art,
Even after climaxing our bodies don't want to part.

Copyright Kenneth Munene

COLOURS OF LOVE

So multifaceted this word called Love
Its use can sometimes confuse
It speaks to all matters of the heart
But also for our favorite food

We sigh and smile with mmm's and ahh's
Our taste buds bring memories flooding in
Of childhood days and a Mothers Love
Who could heal all ails in her kitchen

The Love of the game, the excitement, the win
That causes the adrenalin to rush
The sweet serenades for a new found Love
The romance that makes you blush

The love of community, friends and colleagues
Inspire to give the best you can
The Love one has for his material possessions
Is different to the Love of a Homeland

They say the joy of being in Love
Is what humans should aspire to be?
In the fullness of Unconditional Love
For the Creator is an honoring to thee

The energy of Love in all its forms
Is ever changing in essence and knowing
Sharing the Love energy wherever you can
Ensures the Love keeps on growing

Don't be afraid to speak this word
Aloud to those you care for
Without expectation of reciprocation
But to let them know they're adored

As we celebrate all the Colours of Love
Let us bask in all its beauty
Connect through this fine common thread
For Earth and for humanity

Copyright Shamain Simeon

SHADES OF LOVE

Love is a lyrical song
Written in different tunes and tones.
The feeling is heavenly compared.
Even if it is complicated.
Love is woven with promises.

Deep in the sea of tears.
Rooted in the heart.
Speaks in candied words of love.
Love is like a labyrinth.

Sometimes we end up on a dead end.
Sometimes we are lost on our path.
But love paves its way to the person we love.
Love is a tangled web of emotions.

In different shapes and forms.
As we conquer the name of love.
Love is divine, a gift from up above.
Love is a magic

Full of fun and trick
It's priceless and worth it.
But the best feeling on earth.
With all the flavors of love

We fight and survive
No matter what are the odds?
We always manage to face the world.
The different shades of love

Like the air, we breathe, needed to survive.
Like the universe, it is beyond words
Love is like a kaleidoscope.

Copyright Janet Licudo

WE CANNOT LIVE WITHOUT LOVE

We cannot live without love,
We can behold patterns of love,
Every day, every moment,
The colours of love, color
Every relationship,
No bond can survive without love.
A daughter's love for her parents,
The bond between siblings,
The relationship of parents and children,
The affection of the extended family,
Every relationship prospers
Only when there is love.
Everywhere in nature you can find
The joyful hues of love,
The birds and bees and butterflies,
All the wonderful creatures of the planet,
Flourish because of love.
Love gives meaning to life,
Love gives meaning to work,
We succeed only when we love what we do,
Poets write because they love writing,
Painters paint because they love their art,
Good teachers are passionate about teaching,
Good doctors are devoted to their vocation.
Love is needed in everything,
Nothing can blossom without love.

SPRING FORTH

I know you
I know you not
Spring came
And winter was shot
Autumn was naked
And summer bit the dust
You waved around
As we watched the sea
Talking to another
Was my anxious knee
A heartbeat
I wasn't ready for
Day by day
I saw your seasons
Never constant
I saw pain, i saw laughter
I saw a girl, i saw a mother
I saw shivers, i saw warmth
I never had a way
Every time i had a clue
I lost it the next day
Another phase emerged
I saw care when i had seen hate
I saw favor when i had seen forgiveness
I saw love when i thought all was lost
I saw beauty when ugliness was the makeup
Never was i prepared
When i had placed a ring
Which is which?
I never know
And I will never know
Because

You are the kaleidoscope of my life
Ever slightly, changing your pattern
Giving a glimpses, pulling my curiosity
And making me chase after pieces that never fit
A puzzle, imperfectly perfect
With many colours
Each one different from the last
And forever, my eyes will watch in awe and fear.

MEMORIES OF YOU

I took a walk by the garden and thoughts of us came flashing by like a river flood.
Many old, painful and pleasant vivid memories filled my mind.
I decided sit by the garden chair that dwelled in the heart of our favorite garden.
Love is a sense of feeling of having a companion to build each other up from the smallest things but necessary space of pain of distance love.
By the garden where i sit until hot chocolate turned cold and i still couldn't describe that smell.
The scent of sunscreen or candy floss and i tossed down my mind by having a sip.
And memories of you unwind through that sip.
And the scent from the garden flipped on my back from my behind and i remembered everything now.
Memories are retentive, highly retentive and legendary eidetic.
I recalled back to mind that ever indulged mawkish feeling of us.
When we played hide and seek by this very same garden.
Behind those ironic daffodils that laid unveiling my love that laid hiding my true sense of love, of your love.
That wistful feeling of you that impossible feeling that i cannot have you here next to me.
A desire tinged with melancholy where i wait pining for your love.
That unbearable lust of an unreachable you.
Frequent cries or more precisely whining. A sentiment of pity to oneself.

I stood up and began to walk by the garden to traipse around the garden feeling like an ant traversing the trunks spying distant flowers that give yet no more interest in them.
A memory distant and far faraway.
I went to sit by the chair sleep had now found its way into me.
As I constantly graved the memories so as to wear away little by little until asleep.

THE A OF LOVE

I met you without makeup;
A mask, a magnet
That made wolves lust
Pretty was your face
Natural and raw
Even the pimples weren't shy
Your laughter was clear
Broken and fair
You never hid your teeth
Your hair was shaggy
Dirty and unkept
You always left your comb
Your ear was a virgin
Awaiting the right words
That would ring on it
Not many came for you
And your mind
Never wondered
A girl, you were,
Naive and hungry
Striking down any bird you found
So were the days
Young and calm
Until i fell into your farm
Harvested into your bar
You kept me for the season
Warm and secure, was my state
Every day is a new
I see hidden sides of you
A glow is your dew.
From far we've come
Tired and bruised since dawn

Waves pulled and pushed till we form
Shifting sands made us run
Together, the breeze, we gone
And your care was the warmth
Our love never shied away
As thunders clapped in array
And for me, strong you remained
But now, you frail no more
Becoming my everlasting ore
A diamond still raw

EXTENDED VERSE

But now, you frail no more
Becoming my everlasting ore
A diamond still raw
Breaking my every spectrum
Beautifying my flaws with bows of rain
Washing my pain away
A new layer per day
Forever at ease, you make
That beauty you remain.

LIFE BEGINS WITH LOVE

It is driven and spin on yarn of love
As far as memories can go behind
Cradled in arms of parents in delight
Personified in most beautiful way to unwind.

Life without love is unimaginable
Akin air, to survive hearty and hale
Running on wheels of deepest love
Life becomes a pleasant journey to traverse
The love we give, love we reciprocate, soothes mind as breeze sublime.

Sans language and knowledge
Undulating betwixt passion and compassion
Tender touch, empathy and affection
A bliss, like warm sunshine without any reason
'Neath the turquoise skies in a palette of colours love adorns life.

Life without love is like flower sans fragrance
During the storms, ups and downs of turbulence
Love gives strength, courage n' tolerance
Joy of rainbow it brings to aching soul
Deeper the love, bigger becomes the paradise.

Unconditional and unseasonal
Singing and celebrating love
Life becomes a beautiful sonnet
It covets everlasting true happiness
Mends broken hearts with tenderness.

As dews on meadows, feeling of loveliness
Billions of smiles it pours in liveliness
Two halves become whole
Passionate words scribe poem
Turns ink into gold.

FACETS OF LOVE

The pleasure expanding the good heart
Magnificent an emotion never to give up
Mother and child wanting not to part
Fitting LOVE in one daily cup.

Father ventures to leave the home
When angels are asleep in many dawns
Slaving hours away in workshop's dome
To providential love his brawn he pawns.

His spirit made strong by the memory
Of songs when he callow and shallow
An angel held his hand to wed destiny
Her vow made him a sweet diurnal hero.

Grown, the children's visit on weekends
A reunion of mirth quickening the mind
An epic family togetherness that blends
The past and present, perfect pictures defined.

The family grows adapting and adopting
Love shared too many in God's fashion
Fitting LOVE in one daily cup addressing
Needs of the times, our new devotion.

No! No children be left behind
Stop any war that separates
The young from parents in fronts mined
Love among men saves and liberates.

A TREASURE TROVE OF LOVE

When I was a little lass
I received a lovely gift
It was a small toy, in which
All elements were adrift

Their reflections in the mirror
Constantly altered design
Every time they shifted place
There was a novel image divine

It's a gadget that mirrors
Different phases of ardor
Romance, affection, platonic love
Have emotional splendor

Parents selflessly love children
Siblings love and adore each other
Friends care for one another and
Support with sentiments tender

Love dominates the universe
Blessed with charm and beauty
It sustains relationships
By performing its sacred duty

Then, there's passionate romance
In its mesmerizing form
That keeps the world going
By conforming to social norms

Every aspect of our life
Is replete with love and longing
It's a kaleidoscope of nature
Having myriad colours thronging

LOVE IS THE KEY

Love is you
Love is me
Love is much more than we perceive
Love is in the oneness with the Universe
Love is within us, even though we search
Love is in our eyes when filled with tears
Love is in shared comfort, reducing fears
Love is in the sadness we feel, without it we wouldn't
Love is in the letting go, when we thought we couldn't
Love is in the stillness, when we're fine to, just be
Love is loud in the joy of shared laughter that's free
Love is in the courage to stand up for what's right
Love is in perseverance to see your future is bright
Love is in the connections that we all make
Love is in the forgiveness when we make a mistake
Love is in the kindness we afford others
Love is whānau, sisters and brothers
Love is in the celebrations, when Love is declared
Love is most definitely meant to be shared
Love is you
Love is me
Love is much more than we perceive
Yes indeed, Love is the key

WITH WINGS OF FEELING, STRONG

When affection grows deep among blood relatives;
Or when affection gets metamorphosed into amorist
Or when enjoyment attains pinnacled satiation is love.
Too much fondling of person, thing or activity;
Intimate wishing of a Word or as zero scoring is love.
Love is an emotion having natural omnipresence;
In varied situations it has manifested difference.
Love as life's pole bases actions, reflected, choices,
Decisions, opinions ....;
Love what one sees of on this earth knows no
conditions;
But real one knows not that;
And literally is out of this mundanely.
To be Godly is to be unconditional.
Love is born of sweet amorist in familial bond;
When amorist attains supremacy in relation
Love takes its wings;
Real love takes its form when self-control is
The domineering emotion.
Love is the Absolute's being;
And takes turns of personal and impersonal;
Love that evolves through self-realization
And discards all boundaries of human Making;
Love when rooted darkly in desires and gratification;
A repulsive force sets in to disharmonize noble nature.
Love does eternally mutualize and reflect;
So to have that every human does thirst.
Love does eternally mutualize and reflect;
So to have that every human does thirst.

DIFFERENT HUES OF LOVE

What is love? Love is a mystery, with so many forms
Oh! Sometimes it creates storm's, blessed from above break norms
Some search for it, like lonely souls, wearing shrouds
Lonely soul with tearful eyes, tears like rain, falling from clouds.
Spread around is color of joy, blooming flowers cover earth
Lonely soul searches love, nimble footed, silently, sees all in mirth
Dries her tears, she has seen love, in lovers eyes
Heard it in lover's heart beats, in a broken hearts sighs.
Love has a rhythm, swing, flows like a river
Hum's as a bee, butterfly flirts, dances in glee on flowers
Embrace each petal, kissing all flowers for their beauty
Love shines in mothers eyes, feeding her child, her Divine duty.
Love of stars, playing with the moon, in starlight
Stars, twinkle, break, and sing symphonies to moon's beauty, whole night
Sun rises, as colourful Dawn fades, departs with tears, as dew, dancing on leafs
In twilight, lovers meet on life's horizon, in an intoxicating embrace, to part in grief.
Lonely soul calls her lover, dressed in bridal finery of stars
She hides in starry veils of clouds, she holds him to her heart
Hearing his heart beats, takes out, her love from hearts vault

Love, shines like a ruby, she places it on his heart, in a tearful embrace, cries her heart out.
Oh, dear always be near, never ever leave me, live in my here forever
Let's embrace be in love forever, till eternity like waves love sea
Love is beyond words, as cupid's darts, strike, join hearts, for a happy meaningful life
Lovers, create a world of their own, happy, loving, living without strife.
When two souls fall in love, destiny plays a magical hand
Attracted like magnets, like opposite poles, though belonging to different lands
Whole Universe conspires to bring them together
Made for each other, think alike, like hand and glove
Blessed always is their true love, from friends, Gods, Divine from stars above.

Copyright Vinod Singh

AN OLD COUPLE AT THEIR SUNSET

An old couple at their sunset
Lived with happiness and good spirit
From the beginning to the end
For a colorful life, love game they played.

Their two hearts whispered to each other
To start a new game, full of fun and cheer
Added multiple color to their love life
Enjoyed several reflections of events.

Their minds read signals of each other
Always allowed the side, that is brighter
Tried to synchronize with reciprocation
Making the game a long lasting one.

Two souls too silently watched the game
Appreciated moves of the two players
A beautiful partnership continued long
A life-long togetherness, went along.

Help and cooperation were nice color
Faith and confidence were brighter
Mutual understanding had a golden glow
During all time of happiness and sorrow.

Putting all these colorful beads together
Two lives designed a kaleidoscope of love
When seen through from different angles
Wonderful patterns reflected, a life beautiful.

Arranging the beautiful pieces of love game
Adjusting mirror angles for nice reflections
A beautiful kaleidoscope of love can be made
Life will be beautiful, a nice journey till end.

Copyright Kishor Kumar Mishra

CHANGING PATTERNS OF LOVE

The heart is sacred ground
Where different patterns and colors of love abound
Some grow beautifully
Watered with tears to stay longer even in memories

Others grow so wildly
That it's hard to believe
How true love can be
Leaves with dreams shattered,

Like a withered flower
Crumpled and tossed by the wind
Filial love, the most comfortable love of all
Ready to catch you when you fall

Shows the best gesture of human kindness
Full of love, hugs and kisses
Always beside you when things go amiss
A heaven-sent bliss

Out of passion comes a love that seems so pure
Sounds wonderful for its love for all
A love offered to everyone
Selfless love true and hopeful

To those who accept life's downfall
In the end, witness
The wonder of love bestowed
'Specially to those who endure

But sometimes passion easily fades
An eager feeling but short-lived
Love is a beautiful emotion
We hold in our heart

Especially when expressed with affection
Though some priorities change
Love still remains

COLOURS OF LOVE

Every relationship builds love, unless if hatred it's seed
Emitting colours in life, giving it the importance it needs
Thus love fills our lives with rainbows, colours all around
Strengthening our relationships, as these rainbows keep us bound

Love is all around, and there to be found
Every day, wherever you are, you don't need to search much far
But all aren't that lucky, and some be so picky
That very few get to feel, that feeling of love, for real

Have you found the love that you've been looking for?
Has it been there, all along?
Smiling at you everyday
Unknown to you, that to their heart you belong

Did you get to see the rainbows?
Have you undergone the different shades of blues?
Have you seen the colours of love?
Have you felt love, in different hues?

Love for that someone special, a miss, or mister
Love for a friend, for a brother, a sister
And some relations, that cannot be described
But forever in your heart, their names inscribed

Love for God, and this world He's made
From animals, when their love's displayed
For our parents, that love so pure...
Every color different, but dear, for sure

A kaleidoscope of love, this life
With so much of love inside
Everyone that you see, who lives in your heart
Contribute their shades, when you turn any side

It has a beauty that cannot be outshone
The colours so warm, despite...
Ranging in vibrant shades and tones...
In every relationship, different, but right

TRUE ESSENCE OF LIFE

Love is undeniably mysterious
An enigmatic strange feelings
Different emotions with one purpose
Only your eyes can see the beauty it brings

Only your heart can hear the beat
Inspiring you to do the impossible
Driving you crazy like a roller coaster ride
Love is a missing puzzle to complete your life

It gives you a hundred reasons to give up
But a thousand reasons to pursue your happiness.
Love, the true essence of our life
It cannot be compared to the wealth of the world

Nor cannot be measured by space and time
A collaboration of surreal and real emotion.
Your world suddenly turns into a magical place
Blooming flowers in a fairytale dreams

A never-ending story of excitement
Spicing with troubles and pain
An antagonist in everyone's novel.
Forgiveness is the fruit of love

Even someone turns your dreams into delusion
Complicated, burdened, revengeful
Love moves to conquer this wound
It miraculously healed the broken heart

Love widens the understanding of the heart
Giving yourself the freedom of letting go
Delivering yourself from indignation
Summoning the fruit of love to conquer
Letting love to rule your life.

Copyright Dolo Rez

THE IDEA OF LOVE

The idea of love doesn't have limits or boundaries
It has many facets; full of shapes and colours
Absence of love renders life a starless night
Its presence brings life, bliss and sunshine.

Everyday throughout our lives, love calls
Doing good deed for someone who stumbles
A smile to cheer a friend, distressed or lonely
Encouraging words for someone who hoped
Desperately.

Love can be happy; it can also be sad
But don't perceive that to love is bad
Though love has its ups and downs
It's always around; so don't worry or frown.

Love is empathy; it builds fellowship and camaraderie
Shows care about others, concerns without envy
It's being sensible of someone's feeling or emotion
Reflects understanding; entrance to other's perception.

Sincere compliment evokes warmth and pleasure
Brings a smile on someone's face; a hearty gesture
Feeling of one's joy indeed you are sharing
Love is not merely a colorless or mediocre thing.

God never changes; neither does His love for us
His love is the fullness of life;
True blessing
Love that is beyond, greater than anything
His kindness, mercies and abounding graces
We are recipients of God's perfect love and greatness.

Copyright Azucena Libiran Gonzales

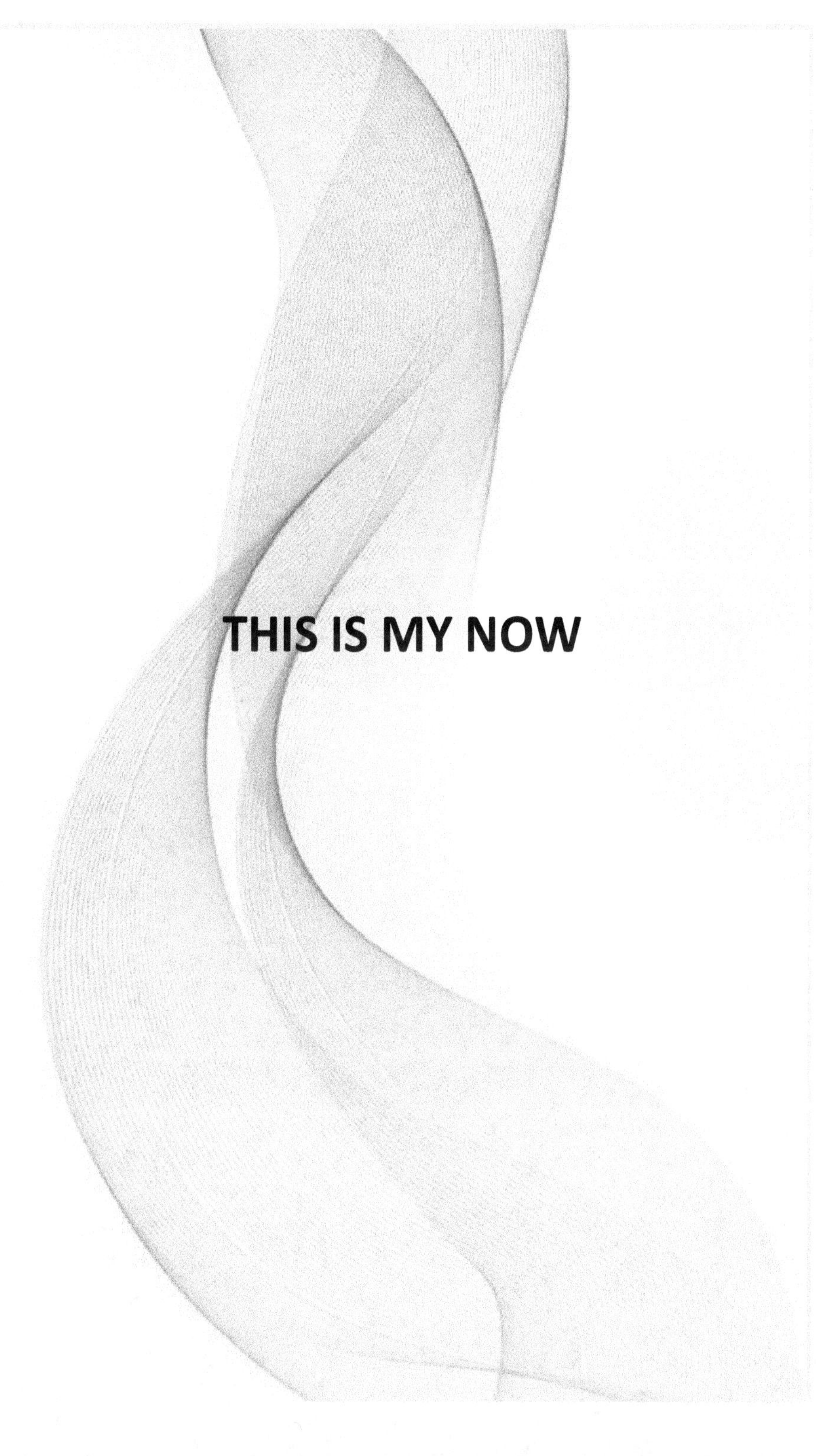

THIS IS MY NOW

EVENING

Mom says the night
To come tonight,
And you are not
Don't they leave you?
Just the way you are
Throw a shirt away
Come on over the moon.
Mom says the night
To come tonight,
Me on Monday
Or without the moon,
Take it
It's night time
It's in the house
You don't know what i am.

Copyright Ollga Farmacistja

WOULD'VE COULD'VE SHOULD'VE

This is your life...
Like a vigilante wanting to free yourself from your crimes...
Battling the ones who truly care...
Giving yourself to those who tear you down and leave you in fear...
Round and round in circles you soon go...
Would've Could've should've never stops...
Let us see how far and deep it truly goes...
Woes upon woes not seeing a future glow...
Only living for today not recognizing your tomorrow...
Time you can no longer buy steal or borrow...
As life now lived leaves you more and hollowed...
Words once used to giving hope and pleasure...
Now the shield in a battle field in a war which you believe you have lost...
Once it was a breeze that helped you rise glide...
Would've Could've should've now the knife that cut your wings...
Putting you in the cage from which you now sing...
Calling for a freedom which never seems to come...
Knowing you cannot fly but with your feet you know you can run...
Song of freedom escape your heart...
For it Sparks' new hopes for those who hears and wish a new start...
Your voice becomes a beacon of hope...
Your cage shall make you free yet...
Would've been better you were free...
Could've been your cage that gave someone their victory...

Should've been a better day but know you will be free someday...
Hold the hope...
Know your worth...
Make your would've Could've should've become a positive...
Not the thing that makes you hurt and distraught...
Free yourself for it is you...
You may be on your own kid...
Happiness reigns always in you...

Copyright Tha Ono

LOVE'S EMBRACE

I yearned to live again
End drab existence
Uproot buried dreams
Curtail ambivalence
Presented my case
Years in isolation
Spirit languishing
Afraid of emotion
Inner bravery judged
Upheld decision
Removed bars
Self imposed prison
I emerged
Felt love's embrace
Fearful me?
Disappeared, no trace

THE LIGHT OF LOVE

Storm of life happens to me
I fall in the eyes of failure
I'm so depressed to be lost in light
The world where I live seem so dark
I am so afraid to find the reality
I have been locked in the loneliness
I feel to live as an outsider
No one knows what I feel
When I open the window of heart
My eyes look the wonderful world
The sun shines to warm life brightly
And white cloud rolls to dance beautifully
I really know nothing for what to do
Just hiding myself in the lonely room
I shout but no one hears me
I cry but no one cares of me
I want to start a new way of life
Where must I begin to do it?
The shadow of bitter memory teases me
As the night mare that follows my step
I really want to move on
Finding the new atmosphere to live
My life feels so meaningless
As the sky has no moon to shine
I hear the heavenly voice to call
It reminds me of true love of God.
God loves those who repent
He gives the light to guide me to the truth
The light of God's love is true
It gives the wings of hope to enter eternal life.

AT THIS TIME HERE AND NOW

Today
Is another day
As of late in the past unfastened
Pushing ahead eventually
This very day a gleaming gift
Another day here we go
One more day of commendable present
To ourselves, genuineness and certainty
Quickly
Whence, comes another fight
Of life's totality
For later
This is my today
What's more, I'm relaxing
At the time
To The Present Time and Place

THE PROMISE

I cannot believe the far that I've come,
Now I have a place to call home,

I had nothing when I started,
I remember how I used to feel frustrated

It's sad when I look into my past,
I thought that poverty would last,

My dreams seemed so far away,
I had no courage to walk the freedom journey,

I thought that I was worthless,
And that I would never taste happiness,

But all that is now history,
I am better than my yesterday,

Looking at all these achievements,
I smile as I cherish these moments,

There are no more tears in my eyes,
No more rain but clear blue skies,

I am glad I never lost hope,
Even though I didn't know of tomorrow's shape,

Look at me now standing on the mountain top,
My joy flowing like a fountain won't stop,

I wake up every morning to kiss the sunrise,
Knowing that I fought so hard to keep the promise.

Copyright Kenneth Munene

MY NEW VISION

I've crossed my rubicon
Burnt the bridge and the lone ship
Let float the letters and icon
Cut the link of bad kinship.

I've journeyed on my own
Feel at home in my skin
Keep a lawn and have it mown
Listen to stories sans sad spin.

I've crossed my rubicon
Burnt the bridge and the lone ship
No more shadow, no more tension
I build reliable relationship.

Let float the letters of desolation
Cut the link of bad connection
No more shadow, no more tension
I have faith in my now and my vision.

Copyright Loreta C Bande

BRIGHTER

I'd look out to the Moon and wish upon the Stars
For ways to change my reality, to heal my aching heart
I'd whisper all my secrets, quietly in the night
Then wait for all the answers to overcome my plight

The tears would start to flow as the months turned in to years
I was ready to give up and drown beneath my fears
That's when I heard the voice, from deep inside of me
Tell me it's been way too long, only you can set you free

You're stronger than you think, remember where you've been
Look in to the mirror, let yourself be seen
For who you really are is more than your despair
You're someone pure of heart, whose always shown you care

Believe in your own power that's brought you to this night
Love yourself as you Love others, fully with all your might
I wept at my reflection and apologized to me
Let go of all I carried and let myself be free

I see me now much clearer, I'd found a new direction
Life has grown much brighter now that I Love my own reflection

Copyright Shamain Simeon

IT'S TIME TO SPARK

Time to shine
Time to be one of them
A mural on the wall of hearts
Beating life into the hopes
Once lost
Once forgotten
Once dejected and rejected
Once grand and fierce
It's time to spark
The moon has been lonely
Without a partner to circle with
Alone in the cold
It's seen all that's come
And will remain after I'm gone
My time is now
Time to place a memory
Not redundant,
Another cliché in the winds of time
Mine has to be different
A tale that must be read.
Regards Mark

TRY NOW

This is my now
How long shall I wait?
How long shall I watch?
As time walks by
Refusing to let me catch it
In pageantry, it's always attractive
Yet the courage within
Never came out of the cave
What if it doesn't go as I wish?
What if I fall? How will i rise?
What if it is not what I want?
What if it's nothing but wind?
Regardless, my time must be now
For too long have I been in the closet
While my skeleton runs free
Absorbing the cold
Falling into pneumonia
Having no cure
And dying in silence
Now this is my now

Copyright Lekeaka McRawlings

TODAY IS BETTER...

Today is better and brighter
Full of sunshine and laughter
With passing of day I bury my past
Now it's time to relax and overcome.

Braving storms as canoe
Holding on to the thread of hope
Scraping out dry tears of past I'm ready to cope.
Sailing towards the light house on shore

It's time to shine as moon
Dissipating darkness strewn
Run amok with bitter memories gone
A new morn awaits to grace upon.
In the present moment

On the present day
My breath assures
I'll feel at ease to hum a new song.

NEW MOMENT

New moment comes
My heart beats
It is significant
For my fresh eyes
I will stay so happy
If I choose love
I will deep in love
Due to my last shot
World seeks justice
This is my now
My moment, sense
My all, my fall
I will stay happiness
If I choose world
Rather I will be goodness
Less to be sadness
My sense and presence
World seeks in my eyes
Time is unbreakable
For my sense

SILENCE IS MY BEST FRIEND

Or rather has become my best friend
When you're gone
Darkness has become my ally.
I stood alone at night, sometimes

Gazing upon the darkened sky
Waiting for a star to fall
Hoping to see your image there.
Gone so long

Gone are the laughter that tickles ones 'heart
Gone are the sweet melodies we played and hum
together
Truly, I wonder
Why the birds keep on singing

The butterflies continue to flutter
Didn't they know how my heart is hurting?
One day, I unveiled my soul
From the gloom I am in

It's been too long, I mourn
A door of hope has opened for me to go on...
You are my yesterday
I am my today
And my tomorrow.

Copyright Lucy A. Mendiola

MOVING ON

I had been in a cocoon for so long
My dreams I left behind, though, they were strong
Afraid of I were about what's coming
Doubts on my mind that's what I was feeling

I should pursue at a moment different
Following a track anew, agreement
O' my mind in trouble, I can refuse
I had had more than enough for a heart

Too much pain along my days were impact
I cried all the tears, walking my destiny
Unfair, life disturbs as an enemy
If we don't play against our own bad fate

What press we down, it will push down full rate
I am thinking about to make a turn
Into happy days, without not much fun
O' my mind in trouble, I can refuse

I had already decided well afresh
Scars of yore I don't see or, hurt and last
I walk a new slow path, beginning small
Hope it goes at large, ever not a fall

If it happens to failing, I won't fade
Days of mine, struggles, for sure, battles made
O' my mind in trouble, I can refuse

THE JOURNEY

The journey is difficult to cross through the crowds
I am not afraid to break the ordinary rules of life
Going through obstacles to reach the peak above the clouds
Watching the chimney's thin plume amid the lovely décor

I am brave and invulnerable
I will be known as the fearless one
Winning all the battles with perseverance.
The happiness and sorrow from the good old days.

Creating a slope to an unending sea quest.
Working to get through the hurdled trail
A stubborn choice I must suffer.
As my yearning falls into the river

At first glance, I felt aghast
It seems the sky is falling apart
Slowly obscuring my entire life
And shedding tears like it is urgent to survive

Leaving me no choice but to undergo the strife.
As the sun sets in the west
The moonlight magnifies the darkness
The tears must now return home

To watch the stars shower of bursting fireworks
Pushing me to uncover the blooming of the flower.
And enjoy life after the struggle.

Copyright Janet Licudo

MY NOVEL INCARNATION

I loved and I lost
Wallowed in the pain
That loss gave me, but
Didn't let my eyes rain

Gathered scattered all
Shards of shattered dream
Kept them safe in heart
With struggles supreme

I have fulfilled all
My duties with aplomb
Now, I, happily
Live sans any qualms

It's new joyous I
Full of life's vigor
I've from past problems,
Taken a detour

I don't cry over
The spilt milk my beau
Not look back to mourn
The time spent with woe

Copyright Sudha Dixit

WHEN I AM MEANINGLESS

In strong complaint/ reproof /counsel /advice...
Or when a new thing develops in me
I feel time loss or nearly so....
I feel as meaningless.
In that imagined world "should" or
"should nets" exist not;
I feel doing what I desire to do;
I do what reflects me or
I do what represents me as my self's
Larger shape;
I feel I start grasping free will:
No matter what I do, I invite no ill will
Blessings overflow my psycho -vale.
Even that material deep pit deflects not
My soul's vision;
I feel freed from greater peril imminent.
The Truth opens its mouth to my feelings
That 'now ' is my good pearl I found
Never to be departed.

ME IN MY NOW

That was a time in the past
I capsuled my hopes and dreams
With disappointment and despair
And put those in a dark chamber.

Unknown fear was haunting me
Felt being buried down the ashes
Rekindling of fire seemed impossible
The time was like losing a battle.

But I rose up from the ashes
Tearing dry earth, Saplings have risen
No more darkness, no more loneliness
All fears gone, I now feel safe.

Sea is still after the tempest is gone
Faith and love swim on Blue Ocean
Sky is clear now, Sun smiles at me
My world is fine, moments are mine.

Copyright Kishor Kumar Mishra

GOD IS ON MY SIDE

It was me, when I'm still in doubt,
That I cannot cross, a river so rough.
But that was when, I have no God,
It's different now, I'm in His charge.

I was then a bird who's afraid to fly,
My wings just folded, whenever I'd try.
But then the sky, provided wind to glide,
Now I can soar, as far as heavens high.

No more a lowly grass, with very little use,
I turned into a plant, no more been abused.
I bloom with flowers, blossom with many hues,
That can tame evil wars, can start any truce.

Not at all a stone, being stepped upon,
Getting bruised and hurt, none gave a qualm.
I can now stand straight, face test with aplomb,
I can be a monument of greatness and calm.

Yesterday was gone, when I do it alone,
God's on my side, steering me to my throne,
He never left me, never was I disowned,
What I am now, He's the one that honed...

And whatever I wish, not at all, I will worry,
What I may become, are all planned for me.
Just like the darkest night, and all black to see,
Sure it'll be over, for morning was designed to be.

THIS IS ME, NEW

You need to believe, never underestimate
Yourself, and don't, for anyone else wait
You'll find your pot of gold, or whatever your future holds
Only if you trust yourself, and take that leap of faith

I wasn't like this before, brave, and so bold
Afraid, to find my way, not knowing what the future holds
But now I've found my way, moving on from yesterday
Towards a better me, my reality, changed manifold

Caught behind in doubts
Being deaf to all the shouts
The screams of my dying dreams
Well this is what my life was about

But not anymore, and surely as it's true
I'm looking forward to more, of this life I never knew
And whatever be my age, I'll never lose my courage
'Cause that was the old me, but this is me... new

And this new me, I love so much more
And not just my love, I find people too adore
The changes I have made, for them a path I've laid
To reach out to their dreams, their future to explore

So look at me now, flowing, like a stream
Don't take me for my flow, I'm stronger than what I've been
Without a hint of shiver, I can turn into a gushing river
That's how I've changed my life, living for my dreams

Copyright Ronel David

NOW I'VE FOUND MYSELF

I blamed myself as I've fallen into the state of misery
Moments when I suffered low self-esteem and extreme uncertainty
Engrossed in the past which seems setbacks are dead end
Wrapped up in the negative, worry kept me burdened.

Lost dreams tormented, crowded my mind with despair
Solitude made me wondering when the day would get better
In quiet reflection, I deemed that failure is not a tragedy
Lack of self-worth and confidence stripped me of liberty.

And then I realized, the wounds didn't shape me
Life's too short to suffer; from the negativity, I must be free
Comforted by the fact that everything happens for a reason
I've sensed the courage to believe in myself and decision.

So I took my blinders off and set myself free
From the ghosts of yesterday, I'd resist and flee
The way to recovery, I'd travel with faith and might
Now I've found myself, I'll rise to my brightest light.

Thank You

www.ingramcontent.com/pod-product-compliance
Lightning Source LLC
LaVergne TN
LVHW010049170826
845678LV00012B/2094